Social Inclusion
in Schools

Also available

Every Child Matters
A Practical Guide for Teachers
Rita Cheminais
978–1–84312–463–4

Social Inclusion in Schools

Improving Outcomes, Raising Standards

Ben Whitney

Routledge
Taylor & Francis Group

LONDON AND NEW YORK

First published 2007 by Routledge
2 Park Square, Milton Park, Abingdon, Oxon, OX14 4RN

Simultaneously published in the USA and Canada
by Routledge
270 Madison Ave, New York, NY 10016

Routledge is an imprint of the Taylor & Francis Group, an informa business

© 2007 Ben Whitney
Note: The right of Ben Whitney to be identified as the author of this
work has been asserted by him in accordance with the Copyright,
Designs and Patents Act 1988.

Typeset in Bembo by Keystroke, 28 High Street, Tettenhall, Wolverhampton
Printed and bound in Great Britain by Bell & Bain Ltd, Glasgow

British Library Cataloguing in Publication Data
A catalogue record for this book is available from the British Library

Library of Congress Cataloging in Publication Data
Whitney, Ben.
    Social inclusion in schools: improving outcomes, raising standards / Ben Whitney.
        p. cm.
    Includes bibliographical references.
    1. Child welfare—Great Britain. 2. Educational law and legislation—Great Britain.
    3. Child abuse—Great Britain—Prevention. 4. Children—Crimes against—Great Britain.
    I. Title.
    HV751.A6W49 2007
    371.7—dc22   2007001566

ISBN 10: 1–84312–474–2
ISBN 13: 978–1–84312–474–0

Contents

Acknowledgements

The views expressed within this book are entirely my own personal responsibility and do not necessarily reflect those of my employing local authority or any of its schools or officers.

I am grateful to Barbara Pavey from NASEN for her support and encouragement throughout the writing process.

Introduction

A very important part of the population we cannot touch at all; I refer to the most degraded of the poor. The children of trampers and beggards. Sometimes, by extraordinary efforts, we get some of these children into school, but they are off again almost immediately; and those are the children from whom a very large proportion of our prisons are peopled. Now the difficulty is, how to get these children under instruction, and how to keep them [there].

(Evidence to the Parliamentary Report on the State of Education, 1834)

I once visited a high school with a mother and her 13-year-old son Adam. We were there for an 'interview' to consider his admission after exclusion from another school elsewhere. We were all three on our best behaviour as we listened to the headteacher's obvious pride in his pupils and their wide range of magnificent achievements, academic, sporting and community. I would have been immensely proud of them too, and their supportive and no doubt, often sacrificial, parents. Anybody would want such a school for their child. Then at last the head turned to Adam and said, 'And what will you bring to our school if you should come here?' 'Nothing but trouble,' said his weary mother, and that was that!

As I approach the later stages of my career in education and social work, I ought to be pretty much exhausted myself, but I am hopeful that this is a particularly exciting time to be doing this kind of work. Perhaps other children and young people like Adam might just get a better deal soon. As the opening quote suggests, we have been trying to make a difference with marginalised children like him for rather a long time.

Teachers and other educational workers, especially those with a particular focus on Special Educational Needs (SEN), will already be familiar with the concept of 'inclusion'. This is a philosophical and practical approach to meeting children's educational needs that seeks, wherever possible, to ensure their participation in mainstream provision alongside their peers. This issue is still a topic of lively debate with supporters on both sides of the argument. There are parents who actively want their own or other people's children educated in this way and others who actively do not. Professionals and politicians are similarly divided. SEN inclusion is a major challenge for schools in seeking to ensure that teaching and learning can address the needs of diverse and often challenging children and young people.

But there is a wider inclusion agenda that is not directly related to SEN as traditionally understood, or in the case of behaviour, that is only sometimes seen in that context. Children's 'needs' are far wider than the strictly educational. They are subject to a wide variety of influences, not only at school. These influences will often be far more significant than their inherent intellectual ability in determining their eventual attainment. Some children have massive hurdles to overcome if they are to benefit from what schools have to offer. They need 'social' inclusion which recognises that these factors, in the child or young person, their family, their local community or society as a whole, may present just as great an obstacle for them as the strictly learning-based issues form for others.

Services for 'vulnerable' children, as they are now usually called, are currently going through unprecedented changes to create a more coherent and joined-up approach that puts the child and their family at the centre. The 'five outcomes' in the Children Act 2004 will be the test of whether these changes are working. Increasing participation in learning and raising achievement are central. The Education and Inspections Act 2006 places a new duty on all schools to promote children's 'well-being'. So what is expected of schools within the government's overall strategy? And, crucially, how does this broader social responsibility relate to the core business of teaching and learning, or is it just an unwelcome distraction?

> Effective schools . . . identify any pupils who may be missing out, difficult to engage, or feeling in some way apart from what the school seeks to provide. They take practical steps – in the classroom and beyond – to meet pupils' needs effectively and they promote tolerance and understanding in a diverse society.
>
> (Ofsted, *Evaluating Educational Inclusion* 2000)

> [The goal is] . . . to have a school system in which every child matters; in which attention is paid to their individual needs for education and well-being; and in which schools can develop the distinct ethos and approaches that maximise the potential of their pupils.
>
> (DfES, *New Relationships with Schools: Next Steps* 2005)

> . . . a system that responds to individual pupils, by creating an education path that takes account of their needs, interests and aspirations, [which] will not only generate excellence, it will also make a strong contribution to equity and social justice.
>
> (DfES, *A National Conversation about Personalised Learning* 2005)

This book aims to provide the busy teacher with the information they will need to be an effective partner in making all this happen. This new emphasis is not about turning teachers into social workers, but there are growing expectations about the range of skills that may now be required within schools. Working with colleagues beyond the school will be increasingly essential. Once we start to address the needs of children in a holistic way, we cannot do it in isolation or be influenced only by our own professional perspective.

The range of topics covered is intended to:

● raise awareness of what is involved in promoting social inclusion in schools,

● stimulate reflection on the questions raised, and

● encourage practical action in making a difference.

This book should also be of value to teachers in training, non-teaching staff in schools, local authority officers, governors and those from a more conventional SEN background who may be taking on wider pastoral roles for the first time. My hope is that, as you read it, real children and young people like Adam from your own experience will come to mind and some new ideas for meeting their needs will emerge.

Key themes

Within each chapter of the book, one key theme is developed in greater detail, as summarised below.

Joined-up services for children

There are new inter-agency tools available such as the Common Assessment Framework, information-sharing protocols, shared databases and thresholds for intervention. All teachers need to have some knowledge of these new arrangements, especially where children are identified as having additional needs beyond what the school can provide. It may not now be appropriate simply to refer the child on to someone else when there are problems. The professionals who already know the child will have a clearer responsibility for making an assessment themselves and identifying new resources with the family. School staff may be asked to act as the 'lead professional', co-ordinating a response to a child's needs from across a range of agencies. What will they need to know in order to do this properly?

Attendance and achievement

School attendance has never been higher up the agenda both for the DfES and for local authorities. It has to be a central focus for daily life in every school. Children who aren't there will clearly be at a long-term disadvantage. Those with SEN need to be there even more than others if they are to achieve their full potential. But should we be tough or tender with parents and pupils? What exactly is the problem? Is unacceptable absence all 'truancy' as it is often labelled or something more complicated? How can schools work with others to combat it? Perhaps we need to make some significant changes to what we have to offer if we are to have any real impact on the eventual outcomes of those who are most likely to stay away.

Exclusion and behaviour

Exclusion from school should be a rarity, not the first line of defence when there are difficulties in managing a child's behaviour. But considerable numbers of pupils find themselves out of school, either for short or long periods, which only reinforces their sense of alienation. There are some children whose behaviour will present as unacceptable, but rarely in isolation from other problems in their lives. What are the duties of schools in the exclusion procedures and how can we strike the right balance between the needs of every child to still receive an education and the rights of everyone else to teach and to learn in a secure and orderly environment?

Safeguarding and child protection

Child abuse never goes away and there has been a renewed focus in education since the death of Lauren Wright and the Soham murders. Being abused as a child is a significant indicator of problems as an adult. What are the responsibilities of schools as part of the new safeguarding arrangements and how can we ensure that vulnerable children are properly protected? School staff must do what is required under inter-agency procedures as frontline children's workers. But can it be done without alienating often hard-pressed and equally vulnerable parents or making their continuing relationship with school even more difficult and creating even more barriers?

Children at risk of missing education

Many children are not in a school or are in danger of missing out on education entirely. Many 'looked after children' in public care, either voluntarily or as a result of court proceedings, may often be out of school as well. What does it mean for school staff that the local authority is a 'corporate parent' for these children, whose lives may have been a whole series of disruptions that has made regular schooling impossible? Other vulnerable groups include children from known marginalised groups like travellers, young offenders, asylum-seekers and refugees and those we have lost, or never known about in the first place. What can we do to ensure that they too have the opportunity to 'enjoy and achieve'?

Making a positive contribution

And underpinning all of this provision is an emphasis on listening to parents and children. This is now supplemented by national and local Children's Commissioners and a range of new duties on service providers. Inspectors will be especially interested in this key area and will ask children and their parents directly what they think of the services we provide. Educators are ideally placed to make a difference for future generations. How might we need to adapt the way we work with families in order to ensure they have every opportunity to take responsibility, even when they are reluctant to work with us? Social inclusion means going beyond blame or negativity into promoting active participation by those who have traditionally been largely disengaged and disaffected. How might we do things better?

To say that 'all children are special' has become rather hackneyed and even slightly politically incorrect. But the ringing theme of government reform of services for children and young people in recent years has been that 'Every Child Matters'. If that is to be true, and in all cases, we need to maintain an ever-wider perspective. We must ensure that education doesn't operate apart from all the other services designed to promote the best interests of all our children and young people, especially those at risk of being left out. It cannot all be done by schools alone but neither can much be done without them. Every child matters and all of every child matters every time.

Resources for obtaining further information beyond the scope of this book, including DfES guidance, websites, organisations, regulations and other key documents, are referred to at the relevant point in the text. The main resources, and a brief selection of other relevant publications, are also listed at the end.

Joined-up services for children

It was like Piccadilly Circus in my house most of the time. There always seemed to be someone there trying to sort out the latest crisis. We had all kinds of people coming round; most of them were OK: social workers, the wag man from school, police, the housing, everyone. Mum dealt with them mostly; she was always up the Social for something, or down the doctor's. I left her to it, or looked after the little ones. It was embarrassing – having to admit that my family wasn't like all the other kids at school. And they never seemed to talk to each other. You'd have to tell them the same stuff over and over again before anything happened. Everyone has problems I suppose, but I always felt different; out of it.

Promoting inclusion

This book is about how teachers and schools can best work together with others to promote the wider welfare of children. More than that, it's about how we must work together in particular for those children on the margins who need us most. Schools are part of a multi-agency network of professionals and services that are intended to bring about an improvement in every child and young person's quality of life and prepare them all for adulthood.

This opening chapter offers an unashamed perspective in support of social inclusion for children within the education system; a 'mission statement' on which all the subsequent chapters will expand. It is based on two simple principles.

- Firstly, that when we say every child (and young person) matters we really mean it, without exceptions.
- Secondly, good or improving outcomes for the majority or even for most children are not a sufficient measure of our effectiveness. We have to be measured against them all. There is a universal entitlement to be delivered and nothing less will do.

We have clearly become more compassionate and inclusive as a society than used to be the case – perhaps we sometimes forget how much things have already changed. My own experience since the 1960s makes the point. When I was at grammar school, I never came across any children with learning problems. They would have all failed the 11 plus and gone somewhere else. If you couldn't cope with the work or, perish the thought, if you misbehaved and the cane or the slipper wasn't enough to make the point, you had to leave and that was that. Most pupils were from middle-class homes like me with supportive parents. Other children from other kinds of backgrounds must have existed, but I never met them, or not at school anyway.

Many previous ways of treating children that used to be seen as perfectly routine have now become unacceptable, such as the right of teachers to hit those in their care. My own children found the very idea incredible. Child abuse was known about for years before it was actively addressed. Similarly, the standards of inclusion that we aspire to now are also higher than before. A greater participation by children with special educational needs is a particular example. Only a generation or so ago they were classed as 'subnormal' or 'retarded', terms now rightly seen as offensive and degrading. That change of attitude has benefited the lives of countless children and their parents.

I began my professional career in the early 1970s. I happened to be one of the first social workers in the new social services departments to concentrate specifically on supporting families with disabled children who had just started attending a school near to where they lived. I was also involved in setting up regular respite care in the community where they, and their parents, could have a break at weekends and in the holidays. This approach, keeping families together wherever possible, was previously almost unheard of but now seems obvious.

I was motivated no doubt in part by the fact that my own, highly intelligent, older brother had muscular dystrophy but unusually, had remained with his family and in mainstream education. If it worked for him, why not for others? Most of his contemporaries were educated quite differently. They didn't live with their families and I saw them only on flag days and at garden parties when they were allowed out from their 'home' somewhere out in the countryside. No doubt they were well cared for and it was, in one sense, a safe and stimulating life for them, but somehow it never felt right.

I have since spent over thirty years in family social work, education and the voluntary sector. I have worked with children in care, churches, parents and community groups and, for the last sixteen years with schools again, this time helping them to engage with another kind of child at risk of being left out: those who may rarely thank us for our efforts and whose lives are in constant chaos. They may seem to delight in breaking all the rules, but their needs and potential as individuals are just as great as those who were overlooked before.

WHO ARE WE TALKING ABOUT?

The original DfES Guidance (Circular 10/99 – *Social Inclusion: Pupil Support*) identified a list of children and young people at particular risk:

- some of those with special educational needs (but not all)
- children in the care of local authorities/looked-after
- some minority ethnic children (but not all)
- travellers
- young carers
- those from families under stress or experiencing abuse
- pregnant schoolgirls and teenage mothers
- poor attenders

To these groups might be added:

- children who are 'missing education' either through formal or informal exclusion or other factors

- those whose behaviour makes them difficult to engage, including those who are dependent on illegal drugs and/or alcohol, young sex offenders and others in the criminal justice system

- other transient groups such as asylum-seekers and refugees

- children with mental health problems

- children and young people living in poverty, who are homeless or whose families are generally marginalised from the wider community

Future generations may yet judge us harshly for our continuing social inequalities, even if they are now rather more subtle. They can still have a significant impact on many children's learning and their subsequent performance and achievement. The assumption that there is now a level playing field available and that all parents and children have a free choice among all schools is clearly a very simplistic analysis. We are not supposed to call them 'league tables' but everyone knows that's what they are. Schools compete, and in any competition there are always losers. Some children are still last to be picked for the team, if indeed, they are allowed to play at all.

For those children who are not easily going to score well in such a competition, achievement and pastoral care are inextricably linked together. Their needs should be at the heart of plans for school improvement. Indeed, at a recent headteachers' conference in my local authority, Steve Munby, Chief Executive of the National College for School Leadership (NSCL), identified how well schools engage with marginalised children and their parents as the first priority for effective leadership in the future and the key to raising overall attainment. These issues must be key priorities for both managers and practitioners in any school, including those that do not necessarily see them as a current priority. They may be missing something crucial.

But schools cannot operate in a vacuum. Children's lives outside school have to be understood and a holistic approach adopted that seeks to meet the multiplicity of their needs, informed not least, of course, by the child or young person themselves. Their own perspective has often been overlooked up to now. It may be helpful to begin by becoming more familiar with the wider 'social care' context within which schools now operate and getting to grips with the language used by others who will be working much more closely with us in future.

KEY DATES IN CHILD WELFARE PROVISION

1872   Infant Life Protection Act

1889   Protection of Children Act

1890   NSPCC formed

```
1933   Children and Young Persons Act
1945   Death of Dennis O'Neill
1946   First recognition of deliberate fractures (USA)
1948   Children Act
1962   First use of term 'battered baby/child' (USA)
1969   Children and Young Persons Act
1974   Death of Maria Colwell
1978   Warnock Report
1981   Education Act (SEN)
1988   Cleveland Inquiry
1989   Children Act
2000   Death of Lauren Wright
2001   Death of Victoria Climbié
2002   Education Act (safeguarding duty ss. 157 and 175)
2002   Death of Holly Wells and Jessica Chapman (Soham)
2003   Laming Report and 'Every Child Matters'
2004   Children Act
2006   Local Safeguarding Children Boards
```

The growth of 'welfare'

Arrangements for promoting the welfare of children in Britain, especially those judged to be most vulnerable, undergo significant change about every twenty years. For the first generation after the war there was a particular need to rebuild family life, literally through improved housing but also through universal health care and expanding employment. But as most of the nation came to accept that we had 'never had it so good', we also had to come to terms with the difficult recognition that some children were not reaping the benefits of the improvements seen by many. This was either through continuing poverty or because of significant shortcomings in the quality of their parental care.

Things were not all as rosy as memories may sometimes suggest. The death of Dennis O'Neill from deliberate abuse and the gradual emergence of 'battered baby syndrome', first in the USA and then in the UK, demonstrated that such issues had not gone away as most must have hoped. Some parents at least could not be trusted with the care of their own children. The privacy and parental authority that was traditionally inherent in British family life now came under much greater scrutiny as the role of the state expanded.

The Children Act 1948 was generally non-interventionist and supportive towards families. In contrast, the Children and Young Persons Act 1969 increased the emphasis on taking children into alternative care. Following the killing of Maria Colwell, both the profession of social work and the need for inter-agency arrangements began to take hold as a largely new element in welfare provision. There was a growing recognition of physical neglect, if often still as a result of poverty as well as intentional cruelty. Then sexual abuse was acknowledged (not in fact new but hardly mentioned, for example, in my own initial social work training). The emphasis was moved away from the previous medical-based therapeutic approaches and on to more practical interventions designed to help families with the problems of everyday living. Social workers in the USA never delivered fridges or gave out grants to pay the rent as I used to do.

Significant numbers of children were now being removed from their parents to live in 'approved schools', 'community homes' and other specialist provision when they were judged to be 'beyond control'. Many children and young people went to Borstals and other punitive establishments when they broke the law. Experts and specialists knew what was best for troubled children, it was thought. Ideally they should be looked after where we didn't see much of them, but where we could also have every confidence that they were in the best place, wherever that was. (It was only in the 1960s that we stopped sending disadvantaged children to Australia.)

Many of those who would now be recognised as having SEN were the most ready victims of such arm's-length compassion. They were deemed 'ineducable' and provided with only the most basic of care in 'mental' hospitals, often in remote, if idyllic, locations. There was little opportunity even for what was usually described as 'training', where it existed at all. We have only had special schools (as opposed to Junior Training Centres) for less than thirty years and in my early working life I would regularly visit children with severe learning difficulties who had spent their whole lives hidden away, often staying there right through their adulthood as well. Such an approach was taken for granted as best for everyone.

Children Act 1989 and beyond

However, crises such as the events in Cleveland, Orkney and other examples where children appeared to have been removed from their families unnecessarily, undermined public confidence in both residential provision and the judgement of professionals. There was also a growing awareness of physical, emotional and sexual abuse by a small number of staff in children's homes and other institutional care settings. Out of sight could no longer mean out of mind as well. There was an emerging consensus around the need to put more emphasis on the rights of the individual again, of both children and their parents this time, rather than just parents as before.

This thinking, along with other questions about how we should handle the implications for children of parental separation and divorce, led to the Children Act 1989 (implemented in 1991). This is still a key milestone with continuing significance. This Act greatly enhanced the need to work in partnership with parents and to avoid, wherever possible, heavy-handed action which may actually make things worse for children. It is, after all, their welfare that is supposed to be 'paramount'. The pendulum now swung back towards the family, admittedly a more varied and less robust arrangement of relationships than used to be the case. In all but a very few cases, staying at home is likely to be better for the child (and less expensive for the taxpayer), than any alternative. It also means that more children with additional needs are likely to remain in their community, and therefore in local schools, as a result. This was the beginning of the social inclusion approach; it is not a recent invention.

Almost twenty years on again and the neglect and murder of another child, Victoria Climbié, has changed things again for the twenty-first century. This was a shocking, if far from unique, case of child cruelty. It gripped the attention of politicians and raised major questions about professional competence and management accountability, rather than only pointing the finger of blame at the people who actually killed her. Unusually, the criticisms of the subsequent Laming Report went right to the top. The focus in child welfare for the coming years will not be so much on the debate about whether the state or parents should decide what is best for children. Either may be appropriate depending on the child's needs and the parents' circumstances. In itself that is as sterile a dispute as whether mainstream schools or special schools are always better than the other. It clearly depends on a number of factors in each case.

What matters now is that the people to whom the state looks for the well-being of its children must act together. We must do whatever is required to promote the best interests of every child and young person as an individual. Professionals must talk to each other and especially to the child, and take note of what they say in making their decisions. We actually have to deliver services for children that make a difference to their lives, not just set up systems and procedures that work for us but which don't actually improve the outcomes for the 'customers'. It's all about outcomes and standards now. We spend billions on education, social care, family services and support for parents and children. What do they, and especially those who need it most, actually get for it?

The Children Act 2004 and the 'five outcomes'

Teachers, and schools, may have traditionally been somewhat aloof from the changes that have been gripping their counterparts in social care and, to some extent, health. After all, we have had our own changes to cope with as Education Acts have succeeded each other like buses in the rush hour. The only constant has been that nothing is constant. But much of this upheaval was at the level of curriculum, organisation and governance, with children themselves rarely the focus of the various initiatives. With the Children Act 2004, not only have the goalposts been moved but we are all being asked to play on a pitch with entirely different lines and with a largely unfamiliar set of rules. It's more like orienteering than any more structured sport; following the signs to see where they lead but with the goal not necessarily yet in view!

The Children Act 1989, while of enormous significance to social workers and to the few people in education seeking to maintain an inter-agency perspective, passed most teachers by with scarcely a ripple. The then Department for Education and Employment did not even produce a circular about it, preferring instead to give support to a little-known Open University publication, separate from the official suite of guidance. Even allowing for the fact that the Children Act 2004 (s. 11) still fails to put the same duty on schools as it places on all other agencies who work with children, this time things will have to change. The duty in sections 157 and 175 of the Education Act 2002 to 'safeguard and promote' the welfare of children means just the same as section 11 means for everyone else, though it is typical that education still has its own separate legislation.

The overall focus has shifted away from us, or even parents, and on to children. It is, at last, their needs that matter most, or so the legislation says. And, in a revolutionary strategy with implications as yet not wholly clear, education, social care workers and health professionals, all of whom may be seeking to meet the needs of the same child at the same time, can no longer do so separately but must, whether we like it or not, do so together. Thinking in separate 'silos' has to go.

There will be one local Children's Plan, one common inspection (Joint Area Review) and one Children's Services Authority or Trust to co-ordinate it all. We are already learning not to talk about the 'local authority' and the 'local education authority' as somehow different when they are, of course, the same thing. But such thinking challenges major assumptions that have held sway for generations about who is responsible for what when it comes to children.

Change began with the 2003 Green Paper, *Every Child Matters* (ECM), which probably had a wider distribution than any other of its kind. From this has come a whole new national strategy and a reorganisation of service provision at a local level which is still unfolding as I write. The rest of this chapter aims to pick out the key elements for those who may not yet be entirely familiar with them. They are the essential framework for everything that follows.

THE FIVE OUTCOMES

- *Be healthy* – This means children and young people are physically healthy, mentally and emotionally healthy, sexually healthy, living healthy lifestyles, and choosing not to take illegal drugs. We also want parents, carers and families to promote healthy choices.

- *Stay safe* – This means children and young people are safe from maltreatment, neglect, violence and sexual exploitation, safe from accidental injury and death, safe from bullying and discrimination, safe from crime and anti-social behaviour in and out of school, and have security, stability and are cared for. We also want parents, carers and families to provide safe homes and stability, to support learning and to develop independent living skills for their children.

- *Enjoy and achieve* – This means young children are ready for school, school-age children attend and enjoy school, children achieve stretching national educational standards at primary school, children and young people achieve personal and social development and enjoy recreation, and children and young people achieve stretching national educational standards at secondary school. We also want parents, carers and families to support learning.

- *Make a positive contribution* – This means children and young people engage in decision-making and support the community and environment, engage in law-abiding and positive behaviour in and out of school, develop positive relationships and choose not to bully or discriminate, develop self-confidence and successfully deal with significant life changes and challenges and develop enterprising behaviour. We also want parents, carers and families to promote positive behaviour.

- *Achieve economic well-being* – This means young people engage in further education, employment or training on leaving school, young people are ready for employment, children and young people live in decent homes and sustainable communities, children and young people have access to transport and material goods, and children and young people live in households free from low income. We also want parents, carers and families to be economically active.

(DfES, *Guidance on the Common Assessment Framework*, 2005)

It's not quite necessary to repeat them every night before we go to sleep, but the government's plans arising from the 'five outcomes' and the subsequent legislation now create a new definition of purpose for us all, wherever we work. All services for marginalised children have to be measured against them and they are integral to the functions of schools and other services. It might feel as if schools have been pursuing their own rather different priorities. It is not always easy to reconcile these expectations with the immediate focus of a traditional SEN strategy, an Ofsted inspection or the direction identified in the 2005 Education White Paper *Higher Standards, Better Schools for All* and the Education and Inspections Act 2006. But Ministers insist there is no conflict: it is 'both/and' not 'either/or'.

There is also a link here to the 'Respect' agenda, given such personal endorsement by the Prime Minister. The language of 'anti-social behaviour' is often more judgemental and strident in tone than the ECM guidance. But this initiative too is at least in part about trying to change the perennially poor outcomes of those children whose families are largely disengaged from mainstream services. We have to be realistic in recognising that these families are not only 'victims' but may well make a significant contribution to their own poor outcomes. I have often been frustrated in my efforts by the very people I was trying to help – we all have. But maybe I would react in much the same way if I were in their shoes. Professionals need to see past the behaviour to the individuals concerned and to seek to provide services in ways that overcome as many of these obstacles as possible. No one can be dismissed as 'undeserving'.

The vision is of children's services that are much more integrated with each other and in which schools have a crucial role to play. Many other services for children besides education may be physically based in schools in future. Some in particular will become extended schools, offering a wide range of family support over a longer day and through-out the year. Teachers must now expect to work in partnership with other colleagues as a matter of routine.

The government guidance, *Every Child Matters: Change for Children in Schools* (2004), was regrettably a rather less substantial document than some of the others in the series. It has not been widely read within education in my experience, but it offers a clear indication of where we are going and makes a number of interesting links with more conventional educational priorities. What is now required is that the best practice in special schools, and in supporting children who have identified SEN in mainstream schools, now needs to be available to all those children with additional needs of a more social kind. (All the ECM guidance can be downloaded from http://www.everychildmatters.gov.uk/)

EDUCATIONAL OUTCOMES

- *Improving performance*. Pupil performance and well-being go hand in hand. Pupils cannot learn if they don't feel safe or if health problems are allowed to create barriers. And doing well in education is the most effective route for young people out of poverty and disaffection.

- *Every child fulfilling their potential*. New inspection arrangements . . . mean that the criteria for school inspection would in future cover the contribution that schools make to pupil well-being. This would be reflected in the school's self-evaluation (SEF) . . . The data used to inform the discussions with School Improvement Partners will help identify how well different groups of pupils are progressing and whether there are barriers to pupils' learning that can be tackled by supporting their wider well-being.

- *Success depends on services working together.* The government expects children's trust arrangements to be developed in most areas by 2006 and all areas by 2008. This will mean . . . involving schools in local partnerships so that [they] can feed their views into local service planning and, if they wish, provide services individually or in partnership; . . . for example, working together to find places for hard-to-place pupils; . . . Local Authorities working closely with schools in fulfilling their duty to promote the educational achievement of looked-after children.

(DfES, *Every Child Matters: Change for Children in Schools*, 2004)

Integrated working

For example, a child with significant learning needs as a result of sensory or visual impairment, obviously needs the support of a wide range of professionals if the teacher is going to be able to work with her to fulfil her full potential. Various specialist contributions may be required from health, social care and elsewhere. It will be essential to work in partnership with the child's parents in order to ensure continuity and to offer them support in managing her at home. Thorough assessment will be required so that there is a clear understanding of her needs and a clear sense of purpose in the various activities being undertaken. These activities will need to be co-ordinated so that the child and her parents do not have to face an array of interventions from different people, none of whom have spoken to each other. Ideally those services will be located together wherever possible, probably at a school, to make it easier for the parents to access them and for information to be shared.

Every Child Matters and the Children Act 2004 extend this thinking to all children 'in need'. This includes those whose requirement for additional services may arise not so much from any physical or developmental disadvantage, but because they have not received very good parenting or are now in the care system. It includes, for example, those who are exposed to various kinds of risky behaviour like drug-taking or domestic violence and those who come from communities where aspirations and expectations are low and poverty high.

The barriers for these children and young people to access what is on offer at school are just as great, if not greater, than those presented to the child who uses a wheelchair for mobility but who finds the way into their local school blocked by a flight of steps. We have made a clear commitment to tackling the second case, with the Disability Discrimination Act to concentrate our minds on to bringing about real change. The Children Act 2004 presents us with the same imperative for all vulnerable children, and is probably even more difficult to achieve.

WHAT'S WRONG WITH THE WAY THINGS ARE?

A headteacher might make a decision to exclude a child permanently from the school, but without consulting first with those other professionals working with that same child who are trying to deal with the effects of years of neglect, low self-esteem and inappropriate parental care. They might have been able to explain the reasons for the behaviour more fully. Could the head's concerns have been dealt with differently in order to avoid the inevitable consequences of an exclusion?

A social worker might approve the movement of a looked-after young person from one foster care placement to another, without considering the fact that the new home is too far from her present school, which she loves, and there are no places at the one round the corner from her new address which also has a different specialism. Wouldn't it have been a good idea to have some prior discussion with colleagues in education?

Health professionals and the police might visit a house where an 8-year-old child is receiving wholly inadequate care but never think to ask themselves what she is doing there at 11.00 in the morning on a school day and whom they ought to tell. That's exactly what happened to Victoria Climbié. Shouldn't the information be shared with those other agencies that may not even know that she is there?

We wouldn't accept such inadequacies and blinkered thinking for our own children, and that for me is the test. If it isn't good enough for some it isn't good enough for any. But working together will not happen unless we do things differently, see things differently and treat every child as seriously as we would want our own to be treated. It cannot depend on how grateful they or their parents are, nor on how deserving we judge them to be. It was inequalities like that which led previous generations to put their embarrassing children out of sight. Now we have a new group who are in danger of being deemed 'ineducable' and we must not make the same mistake again.

Such shortcomings are based in large part on our lack of child-centredness. This concept has been somewhat discredited in strictly educational terms in recent years. We are now seeing a renewed emphasis on personalised learning and greater flexibility to adapt the curriculum to meet the child's capacities and needs, if still within an overall culture that is more target-driven than some would like. But of course the individual child matters; this is education not mass production. There will always need to be a continuing focus on issues of child development and how to teach in a way that recognises that the child brings something to this relationship that may radically affect the outcome. These ideas should come as no surprise.

But there has often been little time for appreciating the wider context in which children spend their lives outside the school and its impact on their learning. How many teachers have never visited the communities where their pupils come from or talked with other professionals who work there? It should be a compulsory part of induction to spend a day with the education welfare officer (EWO) or home–school co-ordinator. How much initial teacher training time is spent finding out about the roles that will be required outside the classroom, from how to mark attendance registers properly to knowing how to contribute to a child protection referral?

If you put the individual child at the centre, not the school, then we need to know how to collaborate with a social worker or health professional to do our own job properly. The child cannot be someone different between 9 o'clock and 3.30 than they are the rest of the time. That's what social inclusion requires and, fortunately, we have new tools with which to do the job. We do not have to invent them.

The Common Assessment Framework

The Common Assessment Framework (CAF) must be in place everywhere by 2008 and is already being introduced in many areas. It provides a set of shared arrangements through which professionals in universal services can work with families in order to promote better outcomes for vulnerable children. Where problems are identified that require a multi-agency response, someone from the school, nursery, a health setting or other service that knows the family will normally be best placed to begin to identify what the child's needs are. They will normally be best able to assess what contribution each agency may be able to make towards meeting them, rather than some other person who is not currently aware of the family.

The Framework has a standard content but is available in various shared formats for local authorities to develop as they wish, including an electronic version (e-CAF). It creates an opportunity for a comprehensive initial assessment of the child's needs and the identification of any more specialist services that could be provided under section 17 of the Children Act 1989. This should result in more informed referrals if they are needed and less of a sense that social workers are the responsibility of all those children with social and family problems that other professionals don't know what to do with. Every child is everyone's responsibility.

The CAF, building on the previous *Framework for the Assessment of Children in Need and their Families*, requires a three-dimensional understanding of the child across broadly defined 'domains':

- development of the child,
- parents and carers, and
- family and environmental factors.

Within each of these domains is a series of sub-headings, intended to help professionals to identify the areas where information will be needed in order to make a realistic assessment of need.

THE COMMON ASSESSMENT FRAMEWORK DOMAINS

Development of the child

- Health: general health; physical health; speech, language and communications development

- Emotional and social development

- Behavioural development

- Identity, including self-esteem, self-image and social presentation

- Family and social relationships

- Self-care skills and independence

- Learning: understanding, reasoning and problem-solving; progress and achievement in learning; participation in learning, education and employment; aspirations

Parents and carers

- Basic care, ensuring safety and protection

- Emotional warmth and stability

- Guidance, boundaries and stimulation

Family and environmental factors

- Family history, functioning and well-being

- Housing, employment and financial considerations

- Social and community factors and resources, including education

With the important exception of child protection referrals where the child or young person appears to be suffering or at risk of 'significant harm' (Children Act 1989 s. 47), concerns about children's welfare will no longer necessarily need passing to social services. It will be for the inter–agency assessment to determine whether a particular response from them is now required. It will be important to use a pre–assessment checklist, agreed among the agencies, so that everyone has a common understanding of the locally accepted definitions of need. This will then determine when the CAF is the correct response to make. This should make sure that everyone understands the process in the same way and reduce the time wasted in inappropriate referrals.

USING THE CAF

A teacher becomes aware that a child has wider family issues that are affecting their development, beyond the strictly educational, that are not currently being addressed. (He/she may have identified SEN as well which the school can deal with.) There is no need to use the CAF if the child's needs are already being adequately met. Or if they can be met by single-agency action, including support services available within the school or other educational specialists such as an educational psychologist. But perhaps the parent has problems with their mental health or alcohol abuse; perhaps the child is involved with petty crime or has responsibilities as a young carer. Perhaps standards of parenting are generally unsatisfactory, but not at the level where the child is at risk of immediate harm or serious neglect that would require a child protection investigation. A range of other professionals may be involved with the family and there is a need to develop a common strategy. This is what the CAF is for.

Clearly a teacher cannot single-handedly address all of the problems a child may have. But the school has an enormous amount of information about the child and the family and someone has to begin the process. Much of that information will be about their academic attainment, but much will be other kinds of information such as those areas explored in the following chapters: the child's attendance, their behaviour at school, who is looking after them at home, etc. But there will be other areas about which staff at the school may know very little; perhaps the child's health history or what is happening about their family's request for refugee status or to be rehoused. The teacher may not be familiar with local service provision for drugs, alcohol, etc. But knowing who is, and making sure these areas are included in the assessment if they are relevant, may be crucial to formulating any realistic plan that will then impact on the child at school.

Making it work

In situations like these, someone at the school, perhaps the headteacher or special needs co-ordinator or, increasingly, a non-teaching pastoral specialist, will need to initiate a CAF, with the parent's agreement and, for older children, with their agreement too. This might be the first new skill that will be required rather than just filling in a form without the child or family even knowing about it. The CAF cannot be used without the parent or other carer being part of it. An assessment will also need the consent of the child/ young person herself where she is old enough to participate in addressing her own needs (see also Chapter 6).

A professional may have to encourage and cajole, even lead the parent or child through the process, but they will have to be willing to participate. The theory is that parents will accept the value of this approach and see it as far less threatening because it does not raise the immediate spectre of their children being 'taken away' by social services or of a negative judgement being made about them. Perhaps surprisingly, this is still the dominant reaction among many families where social workers are involved and seriously militates against parents asking for help, even when they know they need it.

There will then need to be a meeting of all the professionals who know the child or young person, ideally identified by the family. The workers and the family, including school staff, will each contribute the information they have towards making the assessment. They will together identify both strengths and weaknesses in the child's situation and then sign off the assessment as the basis of the agreed needs that can then be matched with local services. No long series of separate appointments and interviews with different agencies. No delay caused by passing the family around like a hot potato in the vain hope that that someone else will 'do' something! Everyone keeps a copy of the assessment and, even if referral elsewhere is still required, it is not being sent out 'blind' but based on coherent and verifiable data that ensures the family is appropriate for the services that agency has to offer.

Of course it won't always be like that! The parent or child may not co-operate, at least to begin with. A key agency may fail to complete the various sections of the CAF. The service that is needed may have a long waiting list before they can respond. The teacher may be too busy to make the meeting. But the current system doesn't always work too well either. There is widespread frustration across the agencies about other people's failure to act as we would like. Far too many referrals are routinely passed over to the social services when there is no prospect of them having sufficient resources to respond, even if it is clear what they could be doing, which it often isn't. This approach moves the emphasis on to us all as part of a common children's workforce and expects us all to work together to develop new services as they may be needed.

People who are not social workers tend to over-estimate both their casework capacity and their power to intervene where children are not being as well cared for as we would wish, but are not at immediate risk of harm. Often they can do little more than make an initial assessment and then, in the face of limited resources and competing demands, close the case because the concerns are not serious enough to justify their involvement. This new process shifts the focus of assessment from 'them' to 'us' and places much more emphasis on intervention now to prevent greater problems later. You don't need a social worker for that. This whole approach must be an improvement for the people who matter most – the children and young people.

Various other initiatives, mostly arising from the Children Act 2004, will be available to support this new way of working:

Director of Children's Services and lead elected member

Local authorities have already begun to put new structures in place that will bring together the management of services previously managed separately in social services and education departments. In many cases this is leading to new locality-based teams which reflect a wider variety of professional skills such as multi-agency support teams, full-service extended schools, children's centres, 'one-stop shops' and other ways of integrating service delivery at the neighbourhood and community level. Not all schools may yet feel part of this process but even if not in an extended school yourself, you should at least notice the difference as the colleagues available to support you with families begin to become part of a more integrated structure.

Information-sharing

A crucial element of the new arrangements is the empowerment of professionals to share information about children and to operate from shared databases. This has proved very complicated in practice. IT systems do not always communicate with each other. There are difficulties imposed by the Data Protection Act and there have been objections from some parents' groups about who needs to know what may be quite sensitive information about their personal circumstances. But progress is being made and at least a limited shared database will be in place shortly, albeit probably local rather than national.

Lead professional

Another key component is the development of the role of 'lead professional' who will co-ordinate the delivery of services from a range of agencies. They will act as a single point of contact for the family in order to help them to understand the system. They will seek to reduce overlap and poor communication between all those involved so that families do not have to repeatedly deal with different people without some co-ordination between them. Parents or even the child may well have a role in choosing who this person will be. School staff, both teaching and non-teaching, will be obvious candidates because of the close contacts that already exist in many cases. Training for this role should be available locally as the CAF is implemented.

Service directories

A service directory is a comprehensive on-line information bank of the services available to children and young people in the local area. It should be easily accessible both to professionals and to the public and should include a broad range of preventive services from providers in both voluntary and statutory agencies. This will help to inform meaningful referrals and enable the outcome of the CAF to be related to what is actually available wherever possible. (However the outcome of using the CAF may be to identify a need for a service that is not available. That will still be an important secondary reason for its use to help improve provision once the gaps have been identified.)

Local Safeguarding Children Boards (LSCB)

All this change started with Victoria Climbié and she was an obvious case where effective child protection procedures were required. There must therefore be, in parallel with use of the CAF, a clear understanding of the procedures to be followed where concerns are more urgent (see Chapter 4). The threshold for such a referral must be clear to everyone. The CAF is not a substitute for a proper investigation under section 47 of the Children Act 1989. But it is intended both to lead to better-quality referrals and to ensure more effective responses to less urgent concerns.

Because of the management shortcomings identified by the Laming Report, new arrangements have come into force from 1 April 2006, replacing the Area Child Protection Committees (ACPC) that had been the responsible body since the 1970s. The LSCB, as part of its overall responsibility for safeguarding across the local authority, will have a legitimate interest in the quality of practice in schools as well as in all other agencies.

Conclusion

Will all this change actually happen? I have been around long enough to have a substantial streak of realism. I know the government doesn't always get all that it wants. The Children Act 1989 has probably never had the full impact that was intended but there does seem to be a genuine will this time. Can we change the way we do things? That will be a major challenge. Busy professionals inevitably react with caution when something that looks like more work comes along.

There are significant tensions with some of the changes resulting from workforce reform in schools about who exactly will do all this. Changing the way some families may have been for generations often feels like an impossible task and will not be done overnight. New initiatives are rarely adequately resourced. These are all genuine objections and reasons to be cautious. But I doubt it will be acceptable for these feelings to become the dominant influence on our thinking. They are just the natural uncertainty shown by any busy person who already has more than enough to do.

A NEW CHILDREN'S PROFESSIONAL?

What we may need is a new professional role entirely, along the lines of the 'social pedagogue' or 'animateur' found in large parts of Western Europe and Scandinavia. ('Animation' – bringing things to life; making things happen, change or move forward.) 'Education' in these cultures is about much more than schools. It is based on a fundamentally holistic concept of children and adults in which the teachers certainly concentrate on teaching, but not in isolation. These high-status occupations combine elements of teaching, social work, child care and counselling with a clear focus on promoting the well-being of the whole person. Their role can even include the sort of work done in Britain by occupational therapists, art and drama therapists or nursery nurses. Other social pedagogues look more like conventional teachers (in France) or more like our social workers (in Holland and Germany). Many are employed in schools and other educational settings. Changes of this kind are already underway in the UK with the advent of the 'Early Years Professional' and other similar roles that bridge traditional agency boundaries.

There is a genuine danger that those who are expected to carry out these wider roles will not be properly equipped to do so, but first we must raise our expectations of what is possible. Resources tend to go to where they are most demanded. Changes in traditional professional status could be involved. Budgets may have to be spent differently and there is never enough to do everything. Systems tend to evolve gradually. But we have to try. We must do better for some of the most disadvantaged children in our society. Schools will have to change even more, and work more in partnership, notwithstanding the organisational pressures from other directions that appear to be encouraging them to become more independent and exclusive, not less.

I ask only that we don't give up on this new approach before we have even tried it. The crucial step is to expand our own personal horizons in order to gain a better grasp of the wider context within which we now have to operate. Those who have an understanding of SEN and the needs of children across a broad spectrum of ability and social circumstance already have a head start. The rest of this book sets out the range of issues in more detail and identifies the variety of other professionals who are as passionately committed to the job that they have to do with children as teachers are to do theirs. It makes obvious sense to tackle these tasks together.

CHAPTER 2

Attending and achieving

None of my family liked school. Dad always said that he never went much and it hadn't done him any harm. It was OK when I was little. Miss Parker used to let me sit with her in the office and do my work there. But I didn't understand what was going on most of the time. I hated high school; they made me wear a stupid uniform and it was all 'yes sir, no sir' all the time. Why did I have to learn French – I don't live in France! In the end I just stopped getting up on days I didn't want to go and mum let me lie in. It was fun, going into town and dodging the coppers. We just said I had the flu or the dog had died! No-body much bothered.

Every absence matters

Missing school is clearly a major obstacle to achievement and is associated with most of the other indicators of social exclusion in adulthood. In one local authority known to me, only one pupil with overall attendance below 85 per cent gained 5 A★–C at GCSE in 2005. This chapter does not focus on the findings of academic research into 'truancy' and its causes, nor is there space to describe in detail all the possible tactics we can use to combat it. These are easily available elsewhere, especially in the many excellent publications by Ken Reid of the Swansea Institute of Higher Education and on the DfES attendance website (see Resources).

Rather I have concentrated on:

● Identifying the different reasons for absence and the need for a more thorough understanding than is often the case;

● Providing the busy teacher with the practical information and advice they need to do the job of monitoring attendance on a daily basis;

● Outlining the more specialist role of the local authority as a key partner with schools in dealing with the more complex cases;

● Summarising twenty key tactics that may be helpful; and

● Some reflective comments at the end about how we need to think more creatively about this issue if we are to make any significant difference.

No matter what else changes in education, one essential remains the same. There are few more important tasks for school staff and their managers (whatever the school's status) than doing their best to make sure the pupils attend. Children miss out if they are not there, no matter how good their teachers are or how accurately their needs have been assessed. For those with a formal statement for their learning needs or disability, unauthorised absence is often not an issue because of the high level of parental commitment and the likelihood of help with transport. But for others, where behaviour is more the focus, together with those children with significant social and emotional needs, it will be essential to do everything we can to ensure they too are accessing what is available.

Teachers rightly feel that they need help in managing these responsibilities. Indeed they may wonder whether attendance is really their problem at all. The assumption that these tasks can just be 'tacked on' to actual teaching, has at least been recognised in recent reforms of teachers' workloads as an inadequate approach and new non-teaching roles are emerging in many schools. The local authority still has a statutory enforcement duty to fulfil as part of its Children's Services functions, as the commissioner of services and as the school's 'critical friend'. But it will probably not offer the level of direct involvement with children and their parents at the casework level that it used to. As more responsibility has been devolved to headteachers, more must now done by schools themselves.

Despite increased non-teaching support and use of information technology, most teachers still have a crucial part to play:

- They will still take the morning and afternoon register.

- They will normally represent the school with parents and other agencies.

- They spend more time with the children than anyone else and need to have an understanding of wider pastoral issues that may affect their attendance.

- They may need to provide work for absent children to do.

- Children will require additional help once they return in catching up missed work, if the effect of the absence is not to be compounded. Life in the classroom might have been rather easier without them, but we have to do better for them than thinking that negative thought.

If we fail to meet their needs here, we may find ourselves with even greater disruption to their learning in future. Not attending school is not just an 'educational' issue. It may have wide-ranging implications for the child's health, welfare and development that may require a response from a range of services beyond the school. Persistent non-attendance certainly meets the criteria for use of the CAF (see Chapter 1). It could even occasionally be seen as a child protection issue, especially if the child has additional learning needs as well.

Figures from the Department for Education and Skills (DfES) released in October 2006 show a mixed picture about school attendance in recent years.

- A reduction in unauthorised absence (i.e. absence without the school's permission), has not yet been achieved. After years of virtual stability, there has been a very slight increase recently but it is still under 1 per cent of all sessions. This rise may be accounted for by schools becoming stricter in their expectations and implementing the regulations more rigorously by recording unexplained and inappropriate absences as unauthorised. As the DfES recognises, it does not necessarily mean more absence; only the reclassification of more absence as unacceptable.

- Twenty-five per cent of secondary pupils had at least one unauthorised absence in school year 2005/6 (the average for these pupils being 14 sessions missed out of 390 compared with twenty-two that were authorised). This was presented by the media as 'a quarter of secondary pupils played truant'. This is not actually true as absences may be classed as unauthorised for a variety of reasons, including those that are nothing to do with the pupil's own actions, such as parents failing to send in a note to cover an illness or an unauthorised family holiday, etc.

- The figure for primary schools was 16 per cent of pupils having at least one unauthorised absence, averaging 8 sessions (compared with an average of 17 that were authorised). The percentage of pupils in primary schools recording at least one unauthorised absence has been rising slightly, though most have very few. Again, this is probably explained by stricter expectations in schools.

- Attendance in special schools and Pupil Referral Units (neither of which are part of the Free School Meal-based target system – see below) is generally lower than for mainstream schools. There are obvious reasons for this, largely due to the complex nature of the children's needs and, in some schools, high levels of unavoidable absences for illnesses, hospital admissions, etc. However, it could be argued that, in what is significantly more expensive provision per pupil compared with mainstream schools, there should be even greater attention given to attendance here. Children still miss out by not being there. It is certainly essential not to become complacent and accept lower levels than are in fact attainable.

Overall attendance in England was 93.32 per cent in 2005–6 (94.24 per cent in primary schools and 92.08 per cent in secondary schools). The total absence picture is probably a fairer reflection of reality than the previous emphasis on just unauthorised absence. More unauthorised absence is not necessarily a bad thing if it identifies the children who need a response rather than masking their difficulties. There is now a greater emphasis on reducing overall absence which, under current government targets, has to fall by 8 per cent by 2007–8 from its level in 2002–3. Progress towards this key target has been largely on track, though there was a dip in at least some areas during 2005–6, largely due to the severe outbreak of winter flu that year. Too many factors over which the school has no control are involved to allow continuous improvement.

As well as the need to deal appropriately with individual cases, the government has placed extensive legal obligations on schools for recording, reporting and publishing information about absence and attendance. This includes the duty to keep daily attendance registers through to notifying termly data to the DfES, providing attendance information for parents and the local authority, and assisting in legal action against parents where required. (Only the end-of-year return in May currently requires a distinction between authorised and unauthorised absences.) Some secondary schools are now also required to put special arrangements in place to monitor their 'persistent absentees' and make returns about them to the DfES every half-term. All teachers need information and awareness if these tasks are to be adequately fulfilled in practice.

Good practice in schools

The Education (School Attendance Targets) (England) Regulations 2005 require every maintained school in England to set annual targets for reducing absence. Targets then have to be submitted to the DfES well in advance, with local authority agreement. Current guidance from the DfES (September 2004) includes a process for target-setting until 2008. Other than for special schools and Pupil Referral Units, targets are related to the school's level of Free School Meals (in 2003). Each school is now set within a median range of schools with similar levels of FSM entitlement. This identifies the maximum expected level of absence.

Regular target-setting should take place with the education welfare officer (EWO) or other local authority attendance advisor and reflect any local authority target or strategy. The local authority's educational performance in meeting children's needs will be evaluated in large part according to whether or not schools have met their individual targets, of which attendance is a key indicator. There should now be a particular focus on schools that are under-performing against the median for their FSM band, rather than using a more general comparison. 'Is our attendance roughly in line with similar schools?' is the key question. However, this change of emphasis has not always been apparent in some individual inspection reports. Schools may still find themselves criticised for rates of authorised or unauthorised absence that are higher than in other very different schools.

The targets should be communicated to all pupils and staff, agreed by governors and constantly monitored. Pupils whose attendance is causing concern should all have individual goals agreed by school with their parents, and of course with the pupil themselves where appropriate. There is not much point in identifying a target if no one knows about it and without a strategy for hoping to achieve it. While the greatest pressures are in the secondary sector, all school staff across all Key Stages and in all kinds of settings are involved in these responsibilities, even those working in Early Years.

Table 2.1 DfES 2008 targets for primary schools (including infants and juniors; and middle deemed primary)

	1	2	3	4	5A	5B
Level of FSM	0%–3.4%	3.5%–7.5%	7.6%–13.9%	14.0%–26.5%	26.6%–37.1%	37.2%+
Median absence	4.4%	4.8%	5.4%	6.3%	6.9%	7.5%
Attendance target 07/8	95.6%	95.2%	94.6%	93.7%	93.1%	92.5%

Table 2.2 DfES 2008 targets for secondary schools

FSM band	1	2	3	4	5A	5B
Level of FSM	0%–4.8%	4.9%–8.5%	8.6%–13.8%	13.9%–24.2%	24.3%–35.4%	35.5%+
Median absence	6.1%	7.2%	8.1%	9.2%	9.9%	10.2%
Attendance target 07/8	93.9%	92.8%	91.9%	90.8%	90.1%	89.8%

The attendance of pre-school children is not compulsory (and staff in these settings must appreciate the distinction in order to avoid challenging parents unnecessarily and without legal authority to do so). But good habits established here can only benefit the child later. School policies are essential at every level, both in establishing good practice and in order to promote as high a level of attendance as possible. The earlier the intervention, the better for everyone.

Understanding absence

The response required to absence depends to a large extent on the nature of the behaviour involved. There are a number of reasons why the child or young person may be experiencing difficulty in attending regularly (beyond the minor incidents that are easily resolved). The absence needs to be carefully analysed:

Truancy

This term is best applied to those who are absent without the support or encouragement of their parents. This may be for whole sessions or when children leave school after registering. Some definitions of truancy do not involve the child even leaving the premises, e.g. avoiding lessons by hiding. This is largely a disciplinary matter, not a question of law enforcement, and is best sorted out with parents. Children do not break the law by such behaviour. Even if the police get involved or if the child is apprehended in the street, there is no offence of 'truancy' for which action can be taken against them. Much can be done by schools to tackle such issues with vigilance, flexibility and imagination. Many children respond to incentives and rewards for improvements but some will not easily do so. Behaviour of this kind tends to be more common among girls than boys. (Boys tend to misbehave more and get excluded.)

Parent-condoned unauthorised absence

If parents are condoning, colluding with or even initiating the absence, this should not be described as truancy. This is a legal matter and persistent failure to act responsibly by parents may be the subject of proceedings against them (not the child), provided the absences remain unauthorised. More absences are under the control of parents than those initiated by children. School staff cannot hope to detect all the examples for which untruthful explanations have been provided, but they must try. This is likely to be a key distinction in coming years. The government is keen to emphasise that parenthood is more about responsibilities than rights, and making sure their child is in school is fundamental to being a responsible parent. Reminding parents that they do have a legal duty will be an inevitable part of any response to unreasonable absences, even if it offends against the understandable wish of school staff not to upset parents.

Emotionally-based school refusal

This is more persistent than truancy. These children do not attend at all or only very occasionally. It is these who will mostly form the 2 per cent 'hardcore' that the government is most concerned about, not the 'truants'. Such refusal is usually an indicator of some deeper problem in the child's personal or family life, including psychological or psychiatric problems, such as depression and anxieties as well as major behavioural or learning difficulties. It may also be a reflection of poor parenting at a significant level, way beyond those who just need a reminder of their responsibilities now and again.

Estimates suggest that mental health problems can be an issue for one in ten children; up to 100 in an average high school. Many can be helped, but a few will have chronic needs over long periods. Some will end up in the care system or on the margins of conventional society. Sending work home or distance learning methods can be a useful way of maintaining contact and reminding them that they are missed, at least for the first few weeks of an extended absence. For some, the support of a formalised Parenting Contract may prove helpful in setting out what the school and parents will both do to improve attendance. Prosecution of parents will not necessarily make any difference. Special educational provision may be required or even alternatives to school such as home tuition, at least in the short term, though in theory this should still equate to a full-time programme (22–25 hours a week). This is not, however, realistic for many of the children and young people concerned.

School initiated authorised absence

It has to be acknowledged that a significant amount of absence is initiated by schools, not by parents or children. Many of these children are among those most at risk of social exclusion. They may have little or no opportunity to be entered for national tests and qualifications as a result. This group includes those who are excluded or sent home, (both legally and illegally); those given extended 'leave of absence' or placed on part-time timetables for behavioural or other reasons; study leave and those who are still on the roll of one school while awaiting transfer to another, even though it has been agreed that their current school is not appropriate for their needs. There is a significant loss of pupils from schools during Y11 in some areas where they are not expected to achieve GCSEs. This is a worrying trend and inevitably reinforces their lack of qualifications and opportunity rather than doing anything to address it.

Managing attendance

It is essential to recognise that the management of attendance and absence is not entirely a matter for individuals to act as they choose. There is a detailed, and in places, highly prescriptive, framework that imposes obligations on parents, schools and local authorities. It is as much an offence for the proprietor of the school to fail to operate in accordance with the regulations as it is for a parent to fail to fulfil their legal duty.

However, while the legal framework, briefly summarised below, is the same everywhere, the way in which it is interpreted by schools and by others will vary widely in practice, despite attempts by the DfES to introduce more standardised expectations. This makes it difficult to say precisely what should happen in every case. For example, the fact that parents can be prosecuted when their children are not attending 'regularly' requires several local definitions. There is no set level of attendance that automatically requires legal action (though 85 per cent is used by many local authorities as the trigger for referral). Even with the use of common computerised registration codes from September 2006, one school may still interpret its power to authorise absence more generously than another. This totally changes the basis of whether there may be any evidence on which the local authority can proceed.

Local authorities do not all resource their support to schools in the same way. There is no national minimum requirement regarding, for example, how many education welfare officers there should be and how they are deployed. There is no nationally recognised qualification and career structure for those doing such work in order to ensure a consistent professional standard. Some schools have employed their own staff to work on attendance issues as well; others have not. Special schools are often not included in the EWO deployment at all, partly because they are not included in the targets, though this may sometimes also betray an assumption that the attendance of some children is still not seen as particularly important.

Some local authorities have devolved at least part of the Education Welfare Service (EWS) to headteachers, individually or in clusters, so that officers can concentrate more on commissioning, statutory enforcement and performance monitoring. A 'one size fits all' approach across an authority is no longer necessarily appropriate. Schools vary enormously in terms of their intake and may need quite different strategies according to local circumstances. Support has to be targeted where it is needed most. Headteachers may create a particular ethos in how such matters are dealt with in their school which may or may not reflect the legal requirements in every detail. This means that most of this chapter is at the level of 'best advice'. It may require some further application in the light of local needs and circumstances.

KEY RESOURCES FROM THE DFES TO SUPPORT GOOD PRACTICE IN SCHOOLS

- *Ensuring Regular School Attendance* (2003)

- *Guidance on Education-Related Parenting Contracts, Parenting Orders and Penalty Notices* (2004)

- *Advice and Guidance to Schools and Local Authorities on Managing Pupil Attendance* (2005). This document, together with various attachments, has replaced Circulars 10/99 and 11/99 *Social Inclusion: Pupil Support*

- The Free School Meals-based targets strategy for 2003–8 (mainstream schools only)

- *Pupil Attendance and Absence Management in School and LEA MIS systems* (0019/2005). This contains the revised attendance and absence codes which must have been in use in every school from September 2006

- The Education (Pupil Registration) (England) Regulations 2006 and the accompanying guidance *Keeping Pupil Registers*, issued in August 2006.

These consolidating regulations made largely minor amendments to previous practice, the most important of which is clarifying exactly when a pupil becomes a school's responsibility. (This may now begin before they have ever actually attended, if they are supposed to be there.) The accompanying document gives detailed guidance on the management of individual cases and should be referred to for greater detail than is possible here.

All key documents are available on-line via: www.dfes.gov.uk/schoolattendance

---

Registration categories

For *every* session, all pupils of compulsory school age on the Admission Register must be marked as either:

- present,

- authorised absent,

- unauthorised absent,

- attending an approved educational activity off site (must be supervised to be counted as present), or

- unable to attend (due to partial or whole school closure or failure in school transport). (This is new with the 2006 regulations and avoids the pupil being classed as 'absent' for these sessions.)

Deciding whether the absence is authorised is the school's responsibility, not the parent's. The school's attendance policy should make this clear. Every authorised absence must show the relevant code for that half-day session. The majority will be for sickness, holidays and other legitimate reasons, but the headteacher and governors should ensure that clear guidance is given to staff and that agreed procedures are actually followed. Senior staff should be constantly monitoring the practice of those with day-to-day responsibility and ensuring that any uncertainties are dealt with properly.

Everything we do should be to encourage the child's attendance and participation, so generally speaking only unavoidable absences should be authorised. This does not mean that any explanation, however inappropriate, that is offered by a parent must be accepted as grounds for authorisation, only those that are justifiable. A written note from parents (which incidentally cannot be legally required, only encouraged) may not be sufficient. It depends on what the note says. If authorisation is used over-generously, this may send a signal to parents and children that attendance is not important and obtaining authorisation for no good reason is easy. This effectively gives them permission not to come and must be counter-productive.

Clear procedures should be in place where staff feel that too many absences are being accounted for by inappropriate parental explanations. It is quite acceptable, indeed it is good practice, to indicate to the parents that absences will not be authorised in future without some additional assurance that the absences were unavoidable. There is no obligation to authorise on request. This may lead to an increase in unauthorised absence as the school imposes stricter expectations. It should also lead to an increase in attendance (the primary objective) as parents and pupils come to see that the school will not simply grant permission without question. It is not necessarily a good thing to have no unauthorised absence at all if authorisation has been given inappropriately.

Registration Regulations 2006

Teachers and other school-based workers need to be aware that most issues in registration and attendance practice are defined by regulation. Key points include:

- The DfES is increasingly moving towards computerised data collection systems with standardised expectations of all schools. But it is important that the use of technology is not seen, in itself, as a solution to problems of poor attendance. It is the interpretation and use of the data that really matters, even allowing for the helpfulness of being able to do the calculations much more easily and the ease of producing an individual pupil's record. It may be extremely helpful, for example, to make a child's attendance history known to their parents on a regular basis. Computerised printouts are ideal for this purpose. Whole-school records may now be printed out annually, not monthly as before as long as regular back-ups are made (reg. 15).

- Both the Admission and Attendance Registers will normally be kept by means of a computer (reg. 4). The Admission Register must include known information about 'parents' and carers as well as the pupils. This should include those with 'parental responsibility' who live apart from their child, wherever possible. Data collection systems must be set up in a way that asks the right questions on admission and updates the information annually. This should include the school the child last attended, if any, and the admission date. The information held by schools will also be invaluable to colleagues in other agencies where information-sharing arrangements are in place or as part of child protection inquiry.

- Regulation 7 defines the headteacher's power to grant leave of absence, including for holidays with parents during term time. There is no automatic entitlement; only discretion to grant leave for up to ten days per school year. It can be less if that is the school's policy. The circumstances should be exceptional for any longer to be allowed and application must be made in advance by the parent with day-to-day care. The child must be 'going away' but the parent does not necessarily have to be going with them. A parent not living with the child, or a grandparent, for example, needs the parent with care to make the application on their behalf. Schools should develop clear procedures on this issue, especially if they have pupils likely to travel for longer periods to maintain family and cultural links.

- Parents are not free simply to remove children from registers as they wish and take them out of school. Unofficial removal from roll at the school's initiative is equally illegal (reg. 8). The regulations define exactly when it may be done. Other unilateral actions mean the child is no longer a 'registered pupil' and changes their status to educated 'otherwise'. It therefore removes entirely the duty on the parent to ensure the child attends and may leave them without provision. Even those children receiving long-term home tuition or in other alternative programmes, if they are still 'registered pupils' for whom the school has been funded, must receive a mark for every session. This is an essential safeguard against losing track of them and records, like all registration, whether the parent has fulfilled their legal obligation.

Daily vigilance by school staff, in accordance with policy and procedures that are well known and acted upon, is likely to make a real difference for most children. This will normally prevent minor issues escalating into much larger ones. The risk of unavoidable family crises or inevitable teenage rebellion makes even the most ordered and functional family, whose children attend the most stimulating of schools, still vulnerable to occasional unauthorised absences.

As is considered further below, such absences are not necessarily an indicator of major family problems or evidence of a developing anti-authority attitude in either the child or their parent. But they may be an opportunity to act now before the risks may become greater once the habit sets in. Some children just skip school occasionally, perhaps showing an entirely natural avoidance of something difficult or less than exciting, without necessarily repeating the behaviour over again. Much use of attendance and absence procedures is just a routine pastoral response and many situations are capable of relatively easy resolution through prompt action by school staff without need for legalistic or heavy-handed responses.

At the very least, schools need to demonstrate clearly that they are on the ball with attendance. All staff need to be:

- aware of what's going on,
- alert to trends and changes,
- focused on improvement, and
- making full use of all the strategies that are available.

None of this happens by accident. If the overall approach throughout the school is right, much of what follows will rarely be needed.

Working with the local authority

Some cases of non-attendance are just the tip of an iceberg in which not being at school is only the presenting problem betraying something much greater underneath. There are many vulnerable children who are not likely to attend school while all else crumbles in chaos around them. These include those whose family relationships are in crisis; those experimenting with under-age sex, drugs, alcohol or other abusive substances; those with major mental health needs; and many children in the public care system; also, the victims of abuse and of discrimination, and those grappling with the implications of homelessness, acute poverty, domestic violence and bullying.

These children are clearly at greater risk than others. Whether the issues are seen as essentially pastoral or because parents or children have repeatedly refused to engage, school staff need to be aware of what else may be available through the local authority that they cannot do by themselves. Of course schools will always try to work collaboratively with parents to raise attendance, including using incentive schemes and rewards, etc. But where absence persists, formal referral to the Education Welfare Service (EWS) may be appropriate under the procedures agreed locally.

THE EDUCATION WELFARE SERVICE (EWS)

All local authorities will recognise that helping schools to achieve high levels of attendance is a primary function of an Education Welfare Officer (known in some areas as Education Social Workers (ESWs)). The school's attendance policy should make it clear to parents that the EWO/ESW is available to assist them with any problems in ensuring that their children attend regularly, but that they also carry powers of legal enforcement if required.

All local authority services, like schools, are under financial pressure and few are able to resource the EWS as they would wish. Most have developed a partnership arrangement with schools that clearly defines the support that is available and the referral procedure that should be followed. Services also have to be targeted at those schools whose attendance is lowest. As individual EWOs may have a considerable number of schools to cover, it is not always possible for them to check whether children with problems have been detected; that is the school's responsibility. Formal register checks may be carried out in addition to receiving referrals. It is essential for key staff to develop an effective working relationship, with a clear understanding of the role of the EWO within a school's overall attendance objectives. An Annual Plan may be especially helpful.

Parenting Contracts and other voluntary interventions

In many situations, even at this more formal stage, difficulties can often be resolved by home visits, casework, etc. undertaken by the EWO at the request of the school. (Referral to the EWO should not require an assessment under the Common Assessment Framework, but may do so if other agencies need to be involved as well.) The cause of the absence and the nature of the problem may be in school, e.g. inappropriate curriculum, un-assessed need, relationships with peers or teachers, etc., as much as anything to do with parents or home life directly. Where parents could do more to help the child, or could do with more help themselves, a Parenting Contract may be suggested if it has not been tried before (see DfES Guidance 2004 above). This Contract can be arranged by the school alone or in partnership with the local authority if wider resources are required.

EWOs may also make use of group work or other interventions. They generally adopt a practical problem-solving approach that attempts to identify the underlying causes of the absence and then to devise strategies to resolve them. Some may be trained in more specialised counselling skills or therapeutic responses. As indicated in Chapter 1, liaison may be necessary with other professionals and agencies where this has not been explored already or changes in educational provision may be recommended. Like school staff, EWOs always prefer to have the parents' active participation. But some families do not face up to issues until the last minute and may need encouragement to see the whole problem in a new, more serious, light. Most families do not like being boxed into a corner by official agencies, and avoiding a negative spiral of blame and criticism will usually be the most likely way to succeed. But it is not always possible.

If progress cannot be made by agreement, or if parents, for example, do not turn up to meetings (as long as they have had every opportunity to do so), consideration will have to be given to the areas of legal action outlined below. This should happen efficiently and when required, though prosecution may be more likely to work as a threat than as a reality. Some parents do not seem to worry as much about courts, fines, etc., as others do. It may make no difference at all to the behaviour of a rebellious or damaged child or if the real issue is about their mental health, their access to learning or the inappropriateness of their current provision.

There are certainly some parents who seem not to care about the effect that missing school may have on their children in the long run. This no doubt often reflects their own poor experiences as children and their own continuing social exclusion that we are now trying to combat. They may need a fresh approach if we are to make progress (see Chapter 6). Assessing the reason for the absence is crucial, rather than jumping to any particular conclusion too quickly.

The law seeks to be realistic in recognising that 100 per cent attendance is not necessarily required, allowing for 'sickness and other unavoidable cause'. Some situations, such as children living in families where the parent's business requires them to travel from place to place, are given special dispensation. There is considerable discretion, given primarily to headteachers but also, to a limited extent to parents, that enables situations which are less than perfect to be regarded as nonetheless satisfactory.

Education can take place away from the actual building in other settings or, increasingly, by means of information technology and distance learning, as well as by traditional methods. However, this should not be seen as an opportunity for schools and parents to, in effect, collude together in allowing pupils not attend when they should do so. That only reinforces social exclusion and does nothing to combat it.

DUTY ON PARENTS

Section 7 of the Education Act 1996 says:

The parent of every child of compulsory school age shall cause him to receive efficient full-time education suitable –

(a) to his age ability and aptitude and

(b) to any special educational needs he may have,

either by regular attendance at school or otherwise.

Attendance law

If a parent chooses to register their child at a maintained, non-maintained or independent school, the child must then attend 'regularly'. A child who comes to school only every Monday might be said to be attending 'regularly', but they are clearly also falling foul of the requirement to receive an education 'full-time'. In effect this means that any session (half day) on which the child is absent without authorisation is technically an offence by the parent. The number of absences needed to justify a legal or even a more pastoral response by the school, is, however, not defined in law. But just a few days of unauthorised absence would probably not be sufficient to prove the child had not attended 'regularly' over an extended period if their attendance is otherwise good. Realistically, the threshold is much higher.

It is important to note that the legal obligation falls entirely on the parent, not on the child. This should influence the way we work with the child or young person involved. It is absence condoned by parents, or, indeed, about which they are powerless but for which they still have to be held legally responsible, which is currently the focus of any enforcement by the local authority. This is often overlooked, or language such as 'taking the child to court' may be used. This is inaccurate and potentially counter-productive.

Any legal action is supposed to be a protection for the child, taken in their best interests, not solely a punishment. While the suggestion has sometimes been made by politicians, headteachers and others that truancy should be an offence by the child, the rhetoric has always given way once the problems of definition have been encountered. This is not to say that missing school may not be a risk factor in care proceedings, especially with younger children, or an issue in a youth justice setting when young people have committed offences outside school. But absence, whether approved by the school or not, is not behaviour for which they can be punished through the courts.

DEFINITION OF COMPULSORY SCHOOL AGE

This changed from 1998, when a single leaving date for all children in the relevant age year was introduced: Education (School Leaving Date) Order 1997 and Circular 11/97 *School Leaving Date for 16 Year Olds.* All those who are 16 on or after 1 September in any given school year, and who are therefore in that year's NC Year 11, can only leave school on the following last Friday in June. In many cases this will be well after the 16th birthday. (The law is slightly different in Scotland.) The leaving date applies to every child in the relevant age cohort, including those educated outside the school system.

At the other end of the age range children must be educated from the age of 5, though technically a parent cannot be required to either admit the child to a school or educate them 'otherwise' until the beginning of the term after their fifth birthday. Many young people will of course have started younger than 5 and continue in education beyond 16+, but legal compulsion cannot be applied to their parents at either point. (In sixth forms, records of attendance may be required to determine entitlement to the Educational Maintenance Allowance.)

Legal powers available to the local authority

School Attendance Orders (Education Act 1996 s. 437–s. 443)

These are for use only where children are not registered at a school but the local authority takes the view that they should be. They are more properly described as 'school registration orders'. They have no relevance in the context of a child who is already a registered pupil but who is not attending. The difficulty of making a parent re-admit their child to a school once he/she is no longer a registered pupil makes it essential that pupils are not removed from a school's Admission Register without a great deal of caution. Deregistration should only happen with the local authority's agreement if no new school is involved. Some of these situations can be unresolved for long periods if schools or parents act without proper regard to the regulations.

Prosecution of parents (Education Act 1996 s. 444(1))

As noted earlier, parents commit an offence if a registered pupil does not attend 'regularly' (s. 444). The term 'parent' in this context includes any adult looking after the child, even if they are not actually related (though not staff from public agencies). Local authorities can only prosecute on the basis of unauthorised absence provided by the school. Enforcement is the responsibility of the authority where the school is (not now the authority in which the child lives as before).

Although the maximum fine under section 444(1) is £1,000, most fines are much lower. Courts must take some account of the parents' ability to pay. No financial penalty at all may be imposed, e.g. a conditional discharge. A greater range of outcomes is now available as a result of the Crime and Disorder Act 1998, including the use of a Parenting Order which places the parent under an obligation to work with the local authority or a member of the Youth Offending Team. This intervention is designed to address the question of school attendance primarily as a means of reducing the likelihood that the child may go on to commit criminal offences in future. However, actual provision for parenting support is not available everywhere and there is no point in making the Order if no local provision exists.

The 'enhanced offence' (Education Act 1996 s. 444(1A))

There is now the capacity for parents, normally with previous convictions under section 444(1), to be summonsed for the more serious offence under section 444(1A) of 'parentally condoned unauthorised absence'. Convictions at this level carry a maximum fine of £2,500 and up to three months in prison. Such sentences are still rare and may not always work at this late stage. Even where they have been used, there have already been examples of parents being prosecuted yet again for a further offence. Everything possible will be tried by the local authority to avoid such an extreme outcome, but there is occasionally no choice if parents prove consistently unco-operative and the child is hardly in school at all. Other solutions will always be preferred if they are available.

Education (Penalty Notices) Regulations 2004

New powers came into force from 2004 (in England only) that have given local authorities the option of formalising their responses to non-attendance but without the need for a court appearance. A Penalty Notice, along similar lines to a speeding fine, enables a parent to discharge their liability by paying a penalty by post. These have been used quite extensively, though payment rates are generally less than half and EWOs have mixed views about their usefulness. The penalty is currently £50 (per child and for each parent) if paid within 28 days or £100 if paid within 42 days. Payment must be made in full, not by instalments and prosecution must still follow if the parent chooses not to pay. A written warning must be issued first, so most local authorities are not using them 'on the spot' but as part of a casework procedure where the parent is deemed primarily responsible for the unauthorised absence and has failed to respond to previous offers of help, attend meetings, etc.

Education Supervision Orders (Children Act 1989 s. 36)

The Children Act 1989 is the framework for dealing with children who are experiencing family problems. This includes both 'private law' (divorce etc.) and 'public law' (care proceedings, child protection, etc., see also later chapters). The Act removed the power of the (then) LEA to apply to have a child taken into local authority care for not attending school and introduced the ESO as a more proportionate response. As these orders give the supervisor the power to give 'directions' to both parents and children, they may therefore be of particular benefit where there is a dispute between the parent and the local authority which results in significant non-attendance. An application for an ESO would enable a court to determine what is in the best interests of the child. However, such action is extremely rare.

Focusing on outcomes

Much of the material in this chapter so far has inevitably been somewhat complex and legalistic, intended for reference when required. That is not, however, how most attendance problems will be resolved. Attendance law is highly detailed in determining how parents, schools and local authorities should respond to absence. Those with responsibility for promoting children's attainment clearly need to know about it and to understand the powers and sanctions that are available. But they are not as great, nor necessarily as effective, as many might have imagined.

If we are serious about tackling most attendance issues, the quality of the relationship between home and school will in fact be far more important. We make progress by consensus in these difficult areas much more easily than we are likely to achieve it by threats, most of which will actually be pretty hollow. Children do not have to come to school, in the sense that no punishment can be applied to them by the state if they do not. In reality, parents do not necessarily feel they must make sure their children go, despite their legal obligation. Very few will be motivated to engage with school primarily because they want to avoid prosecution. Families have a choice of what to do each day, and those whose lives have already been in some turmoil are fully aware of it.

We have certainly become much more adept at handling and interpreting data about absence. This is useful. But trying to reach our attendance targets by changing individual behaviour in the most chronic cases is often a thankless task, which will have little impact in all but the very smallest schools. The effect of improvement in a few individuals will be minimal overall. If the targets are the sole focus, EWOs can probably do more to improve a school's attendance figures by spending 20 minutes with their registers than they will ever achieve by endless hours of home visits and casework with individuals. Most schools make mistakes and some may be significantly over-representing their absence because proper systems are not in place. Authorising everything may appear to suggest fewer problems. But which approach matters more or delivers best value for money? The messages are certainly mixed.

The social inclusion perspective is firmly focused on the individual child and their best interests. We will be judged against the five outcomes in the inspection of local authorities, or we should be. That means better outcomes for individual children, not cosmetic statistical improvements. There are easier ways to raise school attendance totals if that's all we're interested in. Much of our thinking, and much of our analysis, may therefore be misguided. Most real 'truancy', for example, if that's what we're concerned about, doesn't show up as unauthorised absence anyway. If the child registers and then leaves, the session will still be marked as 'present'. It tells us nothing. Going to school is not half as important as what happens when you get there.

EDUCATION VERSUS SCHOOL?

Is school right for every child? There are families from the travelling community, for example, who have chosen to educate their children themselves, outside the system, beyond a certain age and produced well-adjusted, mature and hard-working adults as a result. Of course they have the right for their children to go to a school, to be included in mainstream society and to get formal qualifications, if that's what they and their children want. But the law also requires the education to be 'suitable' to the child's needs, not just what 'we' think 'they' should have. That's social control not social inclusion.

Children from some minority ethnic communities have to balance the rigid British education system, built around traditional Christian holidays, against maintaining their own religious and cultural roots. That sometimes means extended visits overseas outside school holidays to maintain family links, participate in festivals, etc. What is most important in their lives? Why should they be made to feel that they have done something wrong and that they should just fit in rather than having this wider context, crucial to their coming adulthood, properly acknowledged?

These are difficult tensions to resolve. A target-driven focus would suggest that being at school is all that matters, as might a measurement of outcomes based solely on academic results. But is one role of the school system to support parents in what is essentially their responsibility, not the state's? If so, some entirely responsible parents might sometimes consider time spent doing something else that promotes the child's overall development as just as important as being at school. It's 'education' that is the goal, not just attendance: equipping children for life through enjoying and achieving.

This will be heresy to some, but perhaps even occasional cheap trips to Spain in term-time with their family might be just as important for some children's wider development as another week in lessons. It broadens their horizons to go on an aeroplane or stay in a hotel and at least they see there is a life beyond their estate or local area. Perhaps some useful school work could still be done while they are away as part of the agreement but something of value still rubs off just by being there. It might even stimulate children to want more for themselves than their parents have had and raise aspirations accordingly.

The most recent DfES guidance (2006) suggests that any kind of holiday in term-time requires 'special circumstances'. To say also that permission should not be given solely because of lower prices and even that such unauthorised absences might be sufficient for a prosecution is surely unreasonable and even discriminatory. That's all many families can afford. Are they not entitled to holidays at all? To take such a stance where children have otherwise attended as they should risks wholly unnecessary conflict with perfectly reasonable families. It will create even more barriers in the minds of those who already see schools as judgemental and elitist.

So what are we left with as the 'problem'? Some children choose not to go to school sometimes. Some parents fail to make sure their children go as often as they should. A few deliberately keep them away. But many more families simply feel that education is not for them and never really engage with it to any significant extent. They are always reluctant participants, even if the children are physically there. Perhaps we have to accept that some people will choose to put school second now and again. The bigger question is why some parents feel so disengaged from what we believe to be so important for their children's future. They do not all seem to agree with us.

If parents are consistently failing to ensure that their child receives anything approaching an acceptable education, undermining their health and development and refusing to work with those who can make things better, then fair enough, we have to hold them accountable. We should use our statutory powers to intervene if we have to. For a small number of parents this is emotional abuse or neglect and as much an issue of child protection as is making sure their children don't get physically hurt or abused in other ways (see Chapter 4).

But once you start to analyse what is going on in most cases, it is clear that 'absence' is much more complicated than 'truancy' and that hardly anyone is asking why children are out of school. Many parties are involved; perhaps 'us' on this side of the system as much as 'them' looking in from the outside. The almost automatic assumption that it's all down to lazy parents and out-of-control children is hardly ever challenged. We must be absolutely sure that there is nothing else we could have done to make the school experience more worthwhile for the individual child or young person, and, by extension, for their parents.

We have to want their children in our school and be certain that what is on offer meets their developmental needs, their learning styles and takes account of the external obstacles that might be in the way. We must always hope that parents choose schools as the way to educate their child because they see that what's available there is so much better than anything else, not just because they have to. They may still have misgivings or recognise that sometimes their children don't actually enjoy the experience very much, but they should know that such misgivings are understood and that we are all working together to make things better.

But to get to this point we may need to make a few changes along the way. Maybe primary/secondary transition isn't at the right age or school as we know it doesn't work for everyone. There is sometimes a significant falling off in happiness and attendance once children go to secondary schools. It must have something to do with size and loss of a sense of belonging. Many reasonable parents wonder why they should put their children through it day after day. Developing a wider variety of provision for everyone, properly differentiated according to need and delivered according to their personal learning style in different kinds of 'schools', might reduce the sense that what is on offer is not what they really wanted anyway. We have to make the setting for learning so good that it's unmissable! Here are some ideas for making sure that we have done all that we can to reinforce the point.

Twenty attendance tactics

- Try to avoid half-weeks at school in the planning of INSET days and beginnings and ends of terms. Some parents and children will think it's not worth coming in just for a couple of days.

- Send work home when a child is sick for more than one day with a minor illness. It may prompt a quicker recovery!

- Check that absences are not being recorded where an approved educational activity would be more appropriate. If the child is in a supervised educational setting, they're attending.

- Use attendance at school as a theme for numeracy (percentages, fractions, averages, etc.) or literacy (spelling, imaginative writing, etc.).

- Send targeted parents a weekly report on their child's attendance with a suggestion of a reward from them where it's 100 per cent. Don't forget to include those parents who live apart from their children but who may be seeing them at the weekend.

- Remember to invite the parent who works in school hours to any meeting, even if it means having to hold it later, or make sure they get information by post. Many younger boys, in particular, are looking for greater approval from fathers and need them to show an interest.

- Put the best teachers in the classes where absence and disaffection are most likely to be a problem, at least for some of the time. Inspiration may work where threats will not.

- If a child has an early medical or dental appointment, they can still be counted as present if they come in at the first possible opportunity. Reward the parent's effort in getting them in. Half a session is always better than no session at all.

- If allowing children to leave the premises for lunch is leading to problems getting them back in the afternoon, how about employing activity leaders for an hour and keeping everyone busy instead?

- Use morning registration to celebrate birthdays, make toast, give out rewards, choose the star of the week, etc. Make it feel like you really miss out on something if you're not there.

- Try to avoid sending children home as a punishment. Always think of something else that keeps them in school or in some other supervised educational activity.

- Offer individual children an attendance mentor: ideally someone from outside the school, local industry or a student perhaps, who will keep a regular eye on them and support them.

- Involve your governors in the attendance strategy or as part of an attendance panel that meets with parents or pupils. If they don't see attendance as at the heart of the school's ethos, you can't expect the parents and children to do so.

- If children have to be on a part-time timetable for health or other reasons, try to avoid whole sessions or absence. Coming in late or leaving early is much better. It still allows them to get a mark for that session, whereas missing it altogether doesn't.

- Never give the impression that a child who has come in late might as well not have come in at all. They may decide to stay off the whole day tomorrow to avoid the hassle!

- If any current strategy to tackle absence isn't working – change it!

- Be vigilant about unreasonable staff absenteeism or punctuality. Poor role models are bound to make things worse. There shouldn't be one rule for the staff and another for the pupils.

- Include attendance in assemblies and parents' evenings so that everyone hears the same messages.

- Be proactive about tackling bullying – the main reason why children say they skip school or pretend to be ill.

- Try to keep routine family holidays to one week a year rather than two. If families are visiting relatives overseas for extended periods, take the child off roll and readmit them on their return.

- What's the WIIFM factor? What's in it for staff, pupils or parents if attendance improves? A bottle of wine for the teacher whose class has the most improved attendance, or an extra 'free' next week, might make all the difference!

- Don't blame parents, pupils, teachers, or yourself for things that aren't their/your fault. Life is sometimes complicated and we are all just trying to do the best we can. Children make mistakes. Parents fail. Teachers can't do everything. Move on. There's a new day tomorrow.

Perhaps what we need most of all is for all schools to embrace the practice of the best by doing things entirely differently with those parents and their children who do not currently see what education is for. There is plenty of experimentation around, if largely focused at present on Key Stages 3 and 4 because that's where pressures are the greatest and there is greater flexibility on offer. 'Schools within schools' can make being in Year 7 feel more like primary school. Vocational and work-based courses are clearly an option at KS4 that should be available to those who need it at this late stage, but most of the changes probably need to come earlier.

On a wider front, might some children learn best by a mixture of formal school and other educational experiences like activity-based programmes, practical learning or outdoor education right from the word go? Working outside the classroom is, for example, a much more common part of the curriculum in Wales and Northern Ireland than it is in England. Do some children get into formal education too early when they, and their parents, still need an environment more focused on nurturing than learning? How about timetables that can offer flexibility in the times you have to attend school rather than perpetuating the pattern inherited from an entirely different age and social context? Maybe the hours of the school day need rethinking or everyone should move into a more college-type environment at 14+ to stimulate new opportunities. One-year GCSE courses would certainly help those who have missed out to catch up. Why come in Y11 if you have missed most of Y10? Why not more Internet-based schools, self-help schools or courses that operate mostly in the evenings or at weekends?

And then there's what we teach, or rather what children actually learn. Do we have the curriculum we really need to create well-rounded twenty-first-century adults? Children and parents who are not looking forward to even more education after school life has finished often wonder why they need to know most of what we are trying to teach them. What do our children need to know to be successful in our society, and what kinds of teaching should they be offered in order to learn it? What skills do we most need to foster to enable our young people to go on to be self-sufficient members of the community? Are we not still far too wedded to the nineteenth-century model of academic excellence, designed essentially for the few, that simply does not match the needs of a significant number of those who have to go through it? What would make those who are not here more positive? Address some of those issues and maybe they would want to come more than they do now.

Conclusion

An attendance strategy that is mostly about counting heads, and then putting all the blame on to someone else for the ones who are missing now seems like a very simplistic approach to a much more complex issue. Surely, we can find a better way to show that every child does indeed matter? I suspect that how well schools identify the learning needs of their pupils, and how effectively they are then addressed, especially when there have been just a few breaks in attendance, is probably the most important issue in combating absence. Early intervention and speedy responses are essential.

Chronic absence is usually only the symptom of a problem, not its cause. It is often an indicator of unmet educational need as much as wilful failure to engage by child or parent. Getting the provision right will usually make more difference than all the legal powers put together. This is our chance to help this child, and their parents if need be, to see that what we are doing together now is vitally important for what will happen in the rest of their lives.

Unfortunately, some children, and their parents, have realised that it isn't that important, or that's how they see it. They really don't see that school will make much difference in their lives and perhaps, sadly, many of them are right. It's been the same, as they see it, for generations. That's the expectation that we have to change. From the perspective of the bigger picture, if we continue to fail now, the consequences will be more social exclusion, more unhappiness, more poor parenting and an endless cycle of personal and community disaffection. That can never be enough for any child. The job we all have to do for each individual pupil is that important.

CHAPTER 3

Behaviour and exclusions

I was a devil when I was at school; there's no denying it. I hated it. Most of the teachers were useless. They only bothered with the clever ones. They were always on my back over every little thing and in the end I just snapped. I shouldn't have hit him; I know that now. But I was wound up and just lost it. Things were so bad at home then that my mum didn't even bother to go to the meeting about it. She said it was my own stupid fault and I had it coming. I never went to school again. A man came to do some work with me at home for a while then I went to a special unit with other excluded kids. I was off my head half the time. It was alright there but I left just as soon as I could. Who wouldn't have?

The risk of social selection

For me, and no doubt for many teachers, this is where social inclusion starts to bite. We have worked hard to overcome the barriers that prevent some children and young people from attending school as they should. If necessary we have used our legal powers to force their parents into accepting responsibility for the fact that they're not there. We are constantly vigilant about those who disappear after registration. We send text messages to their parents, carry out checks every lesson and even retrieve the pupils from the streets and the local shopping precinct. We have rewarded those whose attendance is highest and those who have improved. We have arranged special alternative programmes and are confident that what we have to offer in this school meets every individual's needs. The children on the fringes are here like never before. And their behaviour is a nightmare. It was so much easier without them!

A caricature of course but not a wholly inaccurate one. The government is right to link improving behaviour and raising attendance together in its national strategy. But it often feels as though they are undermining each other. Schools are mostly large institutions that run primarily on consent. Most of the rules and standards are accepted, if sometimes grudgingly, by the overwhelming majority of children and parents. Most rarely challenge them to any significant degree. The problem is, social and educational inclusion requires us to tolerate and involve those who don't accept the ground rules: those whose lives outside school don't conform to these standards and who are constantly challenging our every word and straining at every boundary. They need education too. It is not as simple as saying, 'here is our school: take it or leave it'.

There have been a series of stories over the years about inspirational headteachers and other leaders who have turned around a 'failing' school where behaviour was historically poor. Many of these are brilliant at what they do and have demonstrated all the commitment that could be asked of them. They have overcome not only what may have been poor teaching and management but also major obstacles presented by the attitudes and lifestyles of the pupils, families and communities concerned. But there is an easier way to 'improve' a school's standards, and some of those given national prominence may have, at least in part, chosen this route. Exclude all those who won't conform or, better still for the longer term, don't admit them in the first place. Create a new school without all the pupils that caused the problems in the previous one.

Of course headteachers and governors are highly sensitive about issues like these. Few people want to work in a school that is struggling and with unco-operative families. Some of the fresh start schools may appear not to have been as 'successful' as others. But perhaps they are still seeking to be community schools and to take all-comers from the deprived areas in which they are set. Other schools may appear to have turned things around in a much more dramatic way. But have they, in effect, become a different school, and for different children? If so, it's hardly a fair basis for comparison.

What has happened to the children and young people who aren't there any more? Who is meeting their needs now? Perhaps they have just been dumped at the doors of other local schools, much to their disadvantage in performance terms. Perhaps they don't now go to school anywhere. If so, no real progress in social inclusion has been made at all. School improvement hasn't necessary delivered an improvement for those who have been left behind. It's always important to look behind the headlines at what is actually happening on the ground.

This was the unspoken issue during the debate on the government's 2006 Education and Inspections Bill. Opposition to the reforms was not about the possibility of a return to academic selection alone. It was also about the possibly unintended prospect of social selection. Those concerns remain, in my judgement. Giving schools more autonomy will almost certainly drive up standards for those who are still there come the GCSEs. But what will it do for those whose behaviour makes it well nigh impossible to contain them until then? Or for those who have already been caught with drugs in the toilets? Where will they go? Local authorities always had to be concerned for every child. Trusts, foundations, individual headteachers and governing bodies only have to concern themselves with those still in their school.

The government also wants schools to set high standards of uniform and behaviour, to enforce 'respect' in the way that most parents want and to show 'zero tolerance' of indiscipline. Classrooms should be orderly and civilised places in which teaching and learning can be the priority, not lion-taming. Ministers are set on giving teachers a clearer role, with increased authority to intervene by clarifying the law on 'reasonable force' and emphasising their right to impose sanctions, even against the wishes of parents. (This may also increase the risk of teachers being the subject of allegations of assault because situations may escalate into actions that are beyond the boundary of acceptable intervention. Training will be essential to guard against this.) This emphasis on discipline sounds entirely reasonable. But will it also create even more possibility for conflict with those children and parents who will fall foul of the higher expectations? Not all those who have every right to be at school will necessarily agree with what will be expected of them.

The challenge

I have to be pretty cautious here. I am not a classroom teacher or a headteacher and I have no wish to tell anyone else how to do their job. What I would hope this chapter will do is to set out the framework within which sometimes very difficult decisions about behaviour should be made. The DfES guidance on exclusion (*Improving Behaviour and Attendance: Guidance on Exclusion from Schools and Pupil Referral Units*, 2006) is supposed to help. Ignoring it tends to cause greater problems for everyone involved.

Like the Code of Practice on Admissions there is a sense in which this guidance is binding but there also seems to be a significant level of variation in how it is interpreted. Not enough people seem to be sufficiently aware of the guidance, and that may well mean that we get into situations that could have been avoided with a little more reflection. The Education and Inspections Act 2006 will seek to ensure that the Admissions Code is complied with by schools, not just consulted (though some have argued that it still has insufficient teeth). The potential removal of a child from the school is governed by just as much regulation as admitting them, and ensuring best practice needs to be given equal priority.

It is interesting that Tony Blair's 'Respect' agenda, aimed primarily at parents, also includes a sharp criticism of 'informal and unofficial' exclusions from schools. Sending a pupil home for more than the remainder of that day, for example, without using proper nationally defined exclusion procedures is not just inappropriate, it is illegal. The DfES has indicated that it intends to take a greater interest in checking that it does not happen. But we all know that it does, either through inadvertent oversight or deliberate practice. This cannot just be overlooked. Autonomy has to be balanced with accountability if children's interests are to be served as is intended. The guidance seeks to strike that balance and to meet that challenge.

However, few people are concerned to promote the interests of those whose behaviour threatens the safety or well-being of the rest of us. There is a danger that almost any action will sometimes be accepted as reasonable in their case. Who is really bothered why the child did what they did? Sometimes not even their own parents are interested. 'Do I really need to worry about what will happen to them after they're no longer my problem? I've got plenty of other children to think about. Haven't they and their parents forfeited the rights that we allow to those who are prepared to be more reasonable?'

The short answer to the final question in particular is 'no'. These children and parents have rights too. It is the mark of a truly civilised society that we do not write off any of our children. That's where we were fifty years ago with children with Down's syndrome or those classed as 'moral defectives'. Some children do not behave well. Some have been damaged by their life experiences since they were too young to have any control over things themselves. Some have a defined disorder such as ADHD or depression, or they misbehave because they simply cannot understand what they are being asked to do. A few pose a significant risk. But there is always a reason for what they do and they too should be treated with the 'respect' as individuals that is said to matter so much. We cannot always hope to prevent them misbehaving and we may not always be able to understand it when they do. We never want to excuse or ignore it. But such children and their parents are still entitled to due process.

Following the exclusion and behaviour guidance carefully will probably bring about the best outcomes for the greatest number of pupils, parents and schools. There are easier ways to manage things of course, or at least it may appear so in the short term, but professionals should never decide what they will do about complex issues on the basis of their own judgement alone. Reference should always be made to an agreed framework that seeks to safeguard everyone's rights and responsibilities based, above all, on the welfare of the child concerned. That is supposed to be our primary concern. Are we confident that we have done everything reasonably possible to secure their inclusion, even if sometimes, sadly, we cannot achieve it? Put it that way round and surely we are more likely to get it right more often?

Leadership

One of the government's core strategies is to increase the quality of school leadership in managing these issues. The National Programme for Specialist Leaders of Behaviour and Attendance (NPSL–BA) offers a strategy for developing greater expertise and increasing the confidence of professionals. Giving staff the opportunity to undertake this training might be seen as a test of whether or not the need has been properly identified and addressed. Many of these skills are transferable from other areas of management but those dealing with pastoral issues are sometimes not seen as needing this level of expertise or status. However, such skills are essential for all those working in mainstream settings, if we are to ask them to undertake such challenging work on our behalf. Those in the front line also need to be properly rewarded for such complex roles, not be seen only as 'baby-sitters' keeping troublesome pupils out of everyone's way. The approaches outlined in the Ofsted report *Improving Behaviour* (2006), where genuine improvements have been made in previously unsatisfactory standards of behaviour, may be especially helpful as evidence of a whole-school approach.

In individual cases, much will probably depend on whether the behaviour is seen as an SEN issue or just as indiscipline. Advice is mixed here. As will be seen below, the exclusion procedure is essentially about sanctions when children have done some-thing wrong. It also requires school staff to avoid using punishment in situations that are actually about unmet learning needs. I would argue that the same must be true where the behaviour is a symptom of illness or abuse. 'Behavioural, emotional and social difficulties' (BESD) can include the child who makes you and other children frightened to be in the same as room as them as well as the child who sits quietly in the corner avoiding eye contact and refusing to participate. Somehow we have to do our best for them both.

Inclusive behaviour management and exclusion prevention

The DfES guidance *Improving Behaviour and Attendance: Guidance on Exclusion from Schools and Pupil Referral Units* (2006) can be found only via www.teachernet. gov.uk and not in a paper format. (It contains numerous links to other useful guidance, websites, etc. and contact numbers for ordering hard copy versions). The guidance is still based on the first document to promote the concept of social inclusion, Circular 10/99, but has been updated so frequently that the on-line version is now the only reliable one. Importantly, most of the first half of the document consists of guidance about how to avoid exclusions rather than how to carry them out! This should be essential reading for all schools in establishing and reviewing their behaviour management policy.

Key themes from the DfES guidance include:

- **A commitment to prevention**

  In most cases exclusion will be the last resort after a range of measures have been tried to improve the pupil's behaviour. A range of strategies should be in place to address the early signs of behaviour which may lead to exclusion.

- **Behaviour needs to be actively managed**

  Schools should have policies, procedures and staff training in place that will both promote good behaviour and prevent bad behaviour. Policies need to be widely publicised so that all pupils, school staff and parents are aware of the standards expected. Schools should apply their behaviour policies in a consistent, and non-discriminatory way.

- **Much can be done and it works**

  Strategies could include: engaging with parents, counselling, a change of teaching set or class, curriculum alternatives at Key Stage 4, temporary placement in an in-school Learning Support Unit or Pupil Referral Unit, assessment of SEN, involvement of an educational psychologist, use of a Pastoral Support Programme, allocation of a Learning Mentor, Connexions Personal Adviser or member of a Behaviour Support Team (BEST), referral to a specific support service, such as the Child and Adolescent Mental Health Service (CAMHS).

- **Decisions should not be made in isolation**

  The behaviour of pupils at school is often driven by complex combinations of social, emotional and health problems, so the involvement of local authority and other services should be carefully co-ordinated. Schools should not act alone, but equally, support should be available.

Behaviour support strategies

Some might say, 'we do all this already, every time, for every child'. But maybe, if we're strictly honest, we don't really, not always. There is an enormous danger in seeing the exclusion procedure as a process that leads inexorably from one step to the next. This is the problem with any behaviour management system that tallies up points or operates on a yellow and red card system. You have to be able to go back as well as forwards. Children and young people have a habit of fulfilling all our worst expectations, and perhaps their own and those of their parents. They get right to the end of the process as sure as night follows day. Any system needs to place just as great an emphasis on diverting them away from the disciplinary process and into something else if this sometimes inevitable progression is to be avoided.

THE STEER REPORT

The promotion of improved behaviour was given a significant boost by the Steer Report, 'Learning Behaviour' (2005). This high-quality analysis, written primarily by practitioners, aimed to strike a balance between clear standards for pupils and their parents, and creating a culture of 'mutual regard' and effective pastoral support. It would be disappointing if only part of this wide-ranging agenda reaches implementation. The more punitive elements, which were about holding parents more to account and clarifying the legal right of teachers to enforce discipline and assert their authority, tended to receive the greatest publicity. But the Report also proposed practical improvements in pastoral care like introducing the Pupil/Parent Support Worker, one of whose functions would be to work closely with pupils at risk of exclusion and to help them continue with school work should a subsequent exclusion become necessary. It must be someone's job to deal with behavioural issues, without being yet another additional responsibility on already over-burdened staff.

A wide range of initiatives to promote better behaviour in schools has been available in recent years, primarily through the Behaviour Improvement Programme (BIP) in 34 local authorities and the DfES National Behaviour and Attendance Strategy. This has enabled participating schools to explore a range of approaches in partnership with each other, local authority officers, consultants and DfES Regional Advisors. Any school wanting to address its responsibilities in a proactive way will be aware of such schemes, though, to be honest, they do not always add a great deal to what we have already known about before, even if they do sometimes generate extra resources with which to do it. (Similar issues can arise with the attendance elements of the Strategy which can sometimes appear primarily to be repeating what local authorities have always tried to do.)

What such initiatives may do is to create an opportunity for self-review and for ensuring that all staff are on board with what senior management are trying to achieve. A whole-school approach, whatever actual technique or programme is adopted, is obviously helpful. I would only stress that any behaviour improvement strategy needs to be child-centred, not systems-centred. As with absence, children misbehave for a wide variety of reasons. It can sometimes appear that behaviour improvement is all about 'them' fitting in with 'us'; it must also be about 'us' gaining a greater understanding of 'them' and why they are behaving as they are.

Pastoral Support Programmes (PSP) or some other behaviour support plan, either as part of an Individual Education Plan (IEP) or free-standing, and specific to that child, should always be explored where persistent misbehaviour is an issue. These must be genuine attempts to make progress, not merely a way of setting the child up to fail by making demands that we know they, or their parents, cannot realistically meet. Exclusion, especially if it may become permanent, is a very big step to take in the life of a child or young person. It has to be the only possible response to that pupil's particular circumstances, not the inevitable consequence of a policy that cannot be varied but which doesn't necessarily relate to the needs of the individual.

For example, I have attended many permanent exclusion appeals to governors over the years where the actual grounds for the decision at this time in response to this particular incident were not clear. Is this one of the few 'one-off' very serious incidents where there is really no alternative, or is it the last straw in a long line of lesser misdemeanours? Has everyone just had enough? That, in itself, may not be enough to justify the removal of the child from the school.

If it was the second reason, persistent misbehaviour, if at a relatively low level as it often was, the school would normally produce mountains of evidence from conduct logs through to details of all the detentions, fixed-term exclusions and other sanctions that had been imposed. These usually demonstrated an increasing lack of success. What was sometimes less obvious was what had been done to try and break this depressing spiral. What additional support or strategies had been attempted to help the child to improve their behaviour along the way and why did they fail? This analysis is a requirement if permanent exclusion is now to be considered necessary in such a case, without one really serious incident that justifies the action on its own.

Schools should routinely use Parenting Contracts, for improving both behaviour and attendance. These are intended as early interventions and aim to formalise arrangements with parents where that may be helpful. They need to show balance: not only what the parent or child is expected to do but also what the school is offering as practical help in moving things forward. It may be necessary for key staff to become more aware of what parenting programmes are available locally, to enhance their own resources in working with parents. It may be helpful to develop a relationship with a regular external provider (see also Chapters 1 and 6). Otherwise it just looks as if we are all going through the motions until the inevitable outcome occurs; we would be just monitoring the behaviour, not actually trying to change it.

Even if it is agreed that the behaviour requires some punishment or sanction, as of course it should in appropriate cases, the DfES guidance offers a number of alternatives to using exclusion that are outlined below. In my experience they are often not fully considered. Many other ways of expressing disapproval will be available that do not have the dangerous consequence of distancing the child from future access to education. It may never have been the intention to punish the child by denying them their right to be properly educated for months on end, but that is often the consequence. Imagination and the time to exercise it are often the key to progress here. Surely the key question is 'what might actually work in helping the pupil, and possibly their parents too, to see that the behaviour is unacceptable?'

Alternatives to exclusion

An exclusion may well be the easiest sanction for all concerned but in itself achieves nothing, except a few days' break for the teachers. The government plans to hold parents more responsible for what the child does during an exclusion, though this is likely to be very difficult to enforce in practice. Many will do little or nothing to ensure the experience has any productive value. Full-time alternative provision for excluded pupils after the sixth day is expected but is surely not yet possible everywhere.

More realistically, a few days, or even longer, spent at home watching MTV is hardly going to reinforce the point on its own. Not having to get up and go to school like your friends; not having to do any supervised work; not even having to leave the house, do not necessarily sound like a range of consequences that some children would actively want to avoid. There are some better ideas around where the focus is on trying to find something positive in the situation, not just removing the child's access to school.

Examples in paragraph 7 of the guidance include:

- *Restorative justice*
  This enables the offender to redress the harm that has been done to a victim, and

encourages all parties with a stake in the outcome to participate. Even if direct redress to the victim of, for example bullying, is not always possible, the offender could still put something back into the school community as a whole. Such an approach might be particularly appropriate where the behaviour has been directed against staff. But pupils caught smoking have been required to run anti-smoking campaigns; those involved with drugs can be expected to explore the health risks and make some kind of presentation or display for their peers. We are trying to cement their sense of being part of the school, not encourage even further their sense that they are not involved in it.

- *Mediation*
  This is another approach that may lead to a satisfactory outcome, particularly where there has been conflict between two parties, e.g. a pupil and teacher, or two pupils. This may require the services of specially trained staff or could be something that older pupils learn to do for one another through systems of peer mediation. They will be doing it all the time, if informally, outside school; falling out and making up again. Some schools have established regular arrangements with a local mediation agency such as Relate to provide this service.

- *Internal exclusion or the use of an exclusion centre*
  Perhaps shared between a number of schools or with the local authority, exclusion centres, providing internal exclusion, offer the opportunity for the pupil to continue their education in a supervised setting where their behaviour can also be specifically addressed, with or without a formal exclusion as well. These should now become more common if the sixth-day duty is to have any impact. My contact with colleagues around the country suggests that resources that have been allocated to schools for such a facility, as with Learning Support Units more generally, have sometimes been spent on something else seen as more pressing. This places the teachers, parents and pupils in a situation in which they are all doomed to fail.

- *A managed move*
  A managed move from one school to another may enable the pupil to have a fresh start. These arrangements need to be made with care to avoid school A thinking that school B has now become permanently responsible for the pupil when the new school didn't realise that was part of the agreement. Parents also have to be given appropriate choices in making such arrangements rather than simply being told what has already been decided. But changes of school often do not make much difference if the problems that led to the original difficulties have remained unaddressed. It may have been about a particular clash of personalities but the real issue may be something that is only compounded by yet another change in what may already be a very disrupted educational history.

- *Pre-exclusion meeting*
  Most local authorities expect headteachers to give colleagues from support services the opportunity to be involved in exploring alternatives before they write the crucial letter to parents. It will usually be difficult to pursue any alternative later if the headteacher has already publicly expressed a view on what should happen. No one likes to be made to look as if they made a mistake once there has been more time for more consideration, so all possible advice needs to be sought beforehand. Even

at such an eleventh hour, there may be alternatives that have not been fully explored or other ways of resolving the issues may yet be possible. In my view at least, such an approach always displays strength of leadership rather than any kind of weakness.

Fair exclusion practice

Even allowing for the best possible practice in prevention, there will be some situations in most schools where exclusion becomes unavoidable. It may be the school's policy not to use exclusion at all – a commendable approach provided it does not result in decisions to remove children by other means that effectively deny parents their right to challenge those decisions. A genuine 'zero exclusion' policy means other ways are always found that do not compound the child's difficulties. This can set the right tone and mean that, in practice, such a response would be rarely be needed anyway.

But most schools will not adopt that policy. Exclusion will have its place as an appropriate sanction, among others. So is it possible to exclude in an inclusive way? It sounds like a contradiction but the DfES guidance offers a number of careful checks and balances that can still protect the interests of the child, even if there is also a need for them, and perhaps their parents, to accept that their actions have consequences.

Informal removal from the school site

There are exceptional circumstances in which individual pupils may have to be removed immediately from the school site. These are very short-term arrangements and paragraphs 23–24 outline the only situations in which pupils may be legally removed without the exclusion procedure.

● *Where a pupil is accused of a serious criminal offence but the offence took place outside the school's jurisdiction*
  There may have to be a balance achieved here between the needs of this pupil and the needs of their victim, if, for example, an alleged sexual assault has taken place against another pupil over the weekend. Clearly it is not appropriate to punish the victim by denying them access to the school and it may be wholly inappropriate for the two pupils to be in further contact with each other. In these circumstances the headteacher may decide that it is in the interests of both the individuals concerned, and of the school community as a whole, for the accused pupil to be 'educated off-site' for a period, subject to review at regular intervals. This is not an exclusion, and full-time alternative teaching provision must actually be made until the situation is resolved.

● *Where a pupil's presence on the school site represents a serious risk to the health or safety of other pupils or school staff*
  In these extreme circumstances, perhaps where a pupil has acted extremely violently, or is out of control, a headteacher may send the pupil home *for that day* after consultation with the parents. According to the DfES advice this should only be done for 'medical reasons'. This is a little unclear, as the assumption that the child has a medical problem (i.e. a mental or psychological illness) could not necessarily be made at this early stage. I think the intention is to ask headteachers to distinguish between the 'bad', the 'sad' and the 'mad' when a pupil has done something wrong. Non-disciplinary pastoral and therapeutic responses may be more appropriate than automatically seeing the child as misbehaving.

Sending individual pupils home for any other reason without formal exclusion (other than because the boiler has broken down, the teaching staff have been struck by flu, etc.) is not permitted (para. 22). No 'cooling off period' until next week; no 'wait at home until your parents contact me'; no 'stay at home until the meeting after half term'. Neither should parents ever be invited to stop sending the child to school while they 'look for a new school that can better meet his needs'. Nor should the child 'have work sent home' until some unspecified point in the future when some other provision or special school will be found for them by the local authority that may well not even know about them at this point.

This is often a tough standard in practice and I have heard all the reasons why it can't be met. Flexibility is sometimes helpful. But we have a significant number of children, especially in our towns and cities, who are not engaging in any form of education, with all the consequent difficulties in meeting their needs. This is often because somebody at some point in some school somewhere in the past suggested that they didn't need to be there any more. Maybe no one can actually remember now exactly how we got into this situation. No official 'off registration' procedure was ever followed but the child cannot now be classed as absent or any legal action taken against the parents because no attendance register has been marked for them for months. 'We advised the parent to find another school' means nothing and here we are, nine months later, with no school willing to accept that the pupil is theirs. We have to do better than that.

Formal exclusion

According to paragraph 9 of the guidance, a decision to exclude, even for a short fixed-term period, should be taken only:

- In response to serious breaches of the school's behaviour policy; and
- If allowing the pupil to remain in school would seriously harm the education or welfare of the pupil or others in the school.

Only the headteacher or a teacher in charge of a Pupil Referral Unit can exclude a pupil (or, in the temporary absence of the headteacher, whoever is acting on their behalf). In order to ensure a consistent standard, this decision should not be routinely delegated to Year or class teachers. If the headteacher has not been involved in the incident personally, he/she must still sign the letters and ratify all the decisions at the earliest opportunity. Otherwise there is a very real danger that behaviour in one class will be treated in a very different way from behaviour in another. There must be a whole-school approach to defining what kind of behaviour merits what kind of sanction, managed by senior staff according to a whole-school policy and for which they are accountable to governors.

THE TWO KINDS OF EXCLUSION

1. Permanent exclusion
   In all cases, permanent exclusion must be upheld or overturned by the governing body within 6–15 school days. The parents then have the right in every case to appeal to an independent panel convened by the local

authority that can also uphold or overturn the exclusion. Their decision is binding on all parties. If they overturn the exclusion, the pupil must return. The child or young person must remain on roll until this process is completed.

2. *Fixed-term exclusion*

This is for a specified number of school days, up to 45 in one school year. The pupil must return after the specified number of days. An exclusion cannot be open-ended nor can their return be dependent on certain conditions being met, such as the parent attending a meeting or signing some form of 'contract'. For exclusions of up to 5 days in a term, governors have no power to intervene. For those of 6–15 days there need be a governors' meeting at the time only if the parent requests it. They can then uphold or overturn the exclusion if the parent has asked them to adjudicate. For those over 15 days a term, the governors must meet in every case and with the same powers as for a permanent exclusion. There is no right of appeal beyond the governors with any fixed-term exclusion.

The list of 'one-off' offences in paragraph 12, where it may be appropriate to go straight to permanent exclusion, has given headteachers a welcome power to act immediately in response to very serious incidents, even if the pupil has no previous history of bad behaviour. These may include:

- serious actual or threatened violence against another pupil or a member of staff;
- sexual abuse or assault;
- supplying an illegal drug (i.e. not simply possession or own use);
- carrying an offensive weapon (for advice on exactly what constitutes an offensive weapon follow the weblink to the DfES and Home Office guidance: 'School Security – Dealing with Trouble Makers' and the Offensive Weapons Act 1996).

Where such very serious incidents occur, school staff should consider whether or not to inform the police if a criminal offence appears to have taken place. They should also consider whether or not to inform other agencies, e.g. Youth Offending Teams, social workers, etc. This may mean that the disciplinary process then has to be integrated with other action if, for example, the pupil may be prohibited from attending school as a condition of their bail. These instances are not frequent, but they indicate the extreme severity of the circumstances where only permanent exclusion may be appropriate and where no parent could reasonably expect such a decision to be overturned on appeal. The key issue for these children then will be what arrangements exist for their reintegration into education elsewhere. This decision cannot be the end of the educational road, even for them.

Cases of misbehaviour of a less serious kind would normally have to be 'persistent' and 'repeated' to merit permanent exclusion, with a range of other strategies attempted first. Permanent exclusion cannot be justified if they are isolated incidents. One area, for example, that particularly concerns me is the practice of some headteachers in automatically imposing a permanent exclusion where a pupil has made an allegation of assault against a member of staff that has proved to be unfounded. This is not in the list of 'red card' offences. If the allegation is deliberately malicious (not necessarily the same as false, mistaken or unsubstantiated), a fixed-term exclusion may be appropriate. (This of course only relates to malicious actions by the child. If it is the parent who is being unreasonable, action against the child should not even be considered.)

But a permanent exclusion would only be appropriate if this was just the latest example of 'persistent and defiant misbehaviour' and if the child already had a documented history of significant disruption and attempts to address it. It is important not to send a signal that any false allegation (as opposed to malicious) will result in exclusion. It is this perception that a child may themselves get into trouble that inhibits many from telling anyone about the abuse that is happening to them. A few such incidents will involve school staff and they will go undetected if the child perceives that it is wrong to complain about a teacher under any circumstances.

The whole exclusion procedure is intended to preserve the rights of all parties; child, parent and school. It would not therefore be right to remove the parent's right to appeal outside the school about a decision so far-reaching as a permanent exclusion, as some have suggested. Any system needs to ensure fairness and governors cannot always bring the objectivity that may be required. The overwhelming majority of headteachers' exclusion decisions, well over 90 per cent, are upheld by governors or subsequent appeal panels. But people do sometimes make mistakes in the heat of the moment or a headteacher may find themselves under pressure to take a certain action which, with hindsight, could have been avoided and their decision is not really justified. None of us can be above contradiction or considered infallible.

Special cases

The DfES guidance suggests that for some children there should always be a better way. Permanent exclusion may look like a solution but of course it only creates more problems, in the end, for us all. Exclusion should not be used at all for:

> minor incidents such as failure to do homework or to bring dinner money, poor academic performance, lateness or truancy, pregnancy; breaches of school uniform rules or rules on appearance (for example, relating to jewellery, body-piercing, hairstyles, etc.), except where these are persistent and in open defiance of such rules, or to punish pupils for the behaviour of their parents, for example where parents refuse, or are unable, to attend a meeting (para. 21).

It needs only a moment's thought to see that excluding a child for not attending or truanting, for example, is not likely to be helpful, though I have often seen it included in the behaviour log presented to governors as part of the evidence. Arguments over uniform and hairstyles are irritating to everyone but being in school is surely what matters more. As suggested earlier, there are other forms of punishment and other sanctions that would be more suitable in circumstances like these. Exclusion denies the child access to proper opportunity for learning and this should always be the last resort. We want them to 'enjoy and achieve'; we don't want to give them even more reasons not to.

Other than in the most exceptional circumstances, headteachers should avoid permanently excluding pupils with statements of SEN (paras. 45–48). These children are the responsibility of the local authority, not only of the school. Staff should also make every effort to avoid excluding pupils who are at School Action or School Action Plus, including those who are being assessed. In most cases, the headteacher will be aware that the school is having difficulty managing a pupil's behaviour well before the situation has escalated. Staff should try every practicable means to maintain the pupil in school, including seeking local authority and other professional advice and support or asking for an urgent review or statutory assessment. There are usually ways other than exclusion in which to raise the need for a change of provision.

'REASONABLE ADJUSTMENTS'

School staff have a legal duty under the Disability Discrimination Act 1995 not to discriminate against disabled pupils by excluding them from school because of behaviour caused by their disability (para. 46). This applies to both permanent and fixed-period exclusions, and the definition of disability covers pupils with 'physical, sensory, intellectual or mental impairments', which may have a significant impact on their behaviour. They cannot be treated less favourably than other pupils without justification. There is a requirement to demonstrate that there are no 'reasonable adjustments' to the school's policies and practice that might have been made to prevent the incident which led to the exclusion. If these have not been considered, exclusions may be challenged through the wider SEN Disciplinary Tribunal (SENDIST) which has a broader remit than the exclusion appeals panels. This concept is not just about making physical amendments if the needs of the child require other kinds of adaptations, for example in the timetable, curriculum or teaching style appropriate to that child or young person.

Similarly, the law places a general duty on all maintained schools to have due regard to the need to eliminate unlawful racial discrimination and promote equality of opportunity. School staff must assess the impact of policies and monitor the operation of those policies on pupils, parents and staff from different racial groups (paras. 52–54). There is evidence that certain minority groups, especially Afro-Caribbean boys, are still significantly over-represented in exclusions, though there has been some recent improvement. Exclusion must be the right, fair and only action available. If adverse impact is identified and this cannot be justified, then the policy and practice should be revised and these kinds of situations may well be subject to further appeal.

Finally, children in public care (looked-after children) are especially at risk of low attainment in school and of all forms of exclusion from education, both formal and informal (see Chapter 5). Their lives are often particularly damaged by constant disruption, and unplanned changes to their educational provision can have enormous consequences. They may even lose their home as well if, for example, a foster placement breaks down as a result of them not being in school. Headteachers should be especially cautious, especially about any permanent exclusion, where children in public care are concerned and try every practicable means to avoid it (para. 55). Any concerns that may suggest the need for exclusion should be fully discussed with the child's social worker or foster carer, the designated teacher for looked-after children and with other professionals outside the school who are involved with the child, before a final decision is made.

Conclusion

This was not an easy chapter to write, without appearing to minimise the very real problems for staff and pupils caused by the bad behaviour of a minority. It may be equally difficult to read if it challenges what may well be very popular and widely held assumptions about what is best for schools and for most children and young people in them. High standards of behaviour are rightly popular with pupils, parents, teachers and the wider community. It is one crucial role of schools to be part of the process of socialisation and the cultivation of attitudes that do not threaten the public good, perhaps especially where parents cannot be relied upon to do that themselves.

But it is the children who misbehave at school and especially those who end up receiving little or no education as a consequence who may then go on to become the disaffected parents of tomorrow and so it goes on. Social inclusion is about breaking that circle, which will eventually make life better for the whole community. Out of sight is not out of mind if the end result is more street crime, more drug and alcohol abuse and more parents who lack the necessary skill and motivation to support their own children's future education.

Just as there has been a greater emphasis recently on trying to understand the causes of absence, which are not all the same, there needs to be a similar approach with behaviour. This is not about making excuses for children or their parents, or about putting all the blame on to schools when things go wrong. But if we manage things as well as we are able, at least they will not end up being excluded because of our lack of understanding or expertise.

This work with the children on the edges cannot all take place in separate units and in distant locations as used to be the case, although some of the most extreme cases will inevitably need this more specialist approach, at least until the child's needs can be reassessed. But there should always be a way back. Eventually we still have to find a home for these children and young people within the same society as everyone else. With only a very few exceptions, they will all become adults living alongside the rest of us before too long. Reinforcing their sense of being different, or part of a counter-culture that has no place in the wider society, cannot be right. But of course I also want schools to be safe and happy places so that everyone can enjoy the experience of being there. I am not sure that we have yet made sufficient progress in getting things right in this most difficult of tasks. I am also sure we have no choice but to keep on trying.

Safeguarding and protecting children

Of course I never liked it, but I didn't know how to stop it. I just couldn't tell my mum. I tried once but she wasn't listening. I wonder now if she knew anyway. He'd always knocked us about; we'd just got used to it. But this was different. It always happened on a Tuesday night when mum was out. He used to tell me when he'd finished how much he loved me and how special I was. I suppose that meant something at the time. After all he was my dad; you're supposed to love your parents. I was terrible on Tuesdays at school, but I never said anything; not to my mates or the teachers. They wouldn't have understood either. I can see now that it's messed me up for years. Nobody wants damaged goods.

The reality of abuse

A child's exposure to abuse and neglect obviously has a detrimental effect on their overall health and development. It is also likely to have a significant effect on wider issues such as their participation in education and their eventual achievement. Imagine what it must be like to have to get yourself to school every morning because your parent does not bother to wake you, wash, dress or give you breakfast. Some 6-year-olds have to manage such responsibilities themselves. Or what must it be like to spend the day at school counting down with dread the minutes until it's time to go home, knowing that he winked at you over breakfast – his special sign that tonight you have to wait in your room before you have a bath because mum's going out. Children do not learn when they are frightened. Abuse hurts, and not just at the time. No wonder the homework wasn't done and the pupil reacted aggressively when the teacher asked where it was.

As summarised in Chapter 1, the current framework for services to support children in need and to protect them from harm has developed through a series of legislative and policy changes over the past half century. The death of Maria Colwell had prompted the first attempt to set up a multi-agency mechanism for communicating concerns, pooling knowledge and planning strategies to protect children and young people at risk through the local Area Child Protection Committees (ACPC).

The Cleveland Inquiry in 1987 brought into sharper focus the difficulty of dealing with both abuse and its aftermath. Many players are involved: parents, children, the police, courts, staff in the caring services, politicians and the general public. In this case, dozens of children in the Middlesbrough area had been removed from the care of their parents on suspicion of sexual abuse. But there was a widespread feeling, at least among the wider community, that some professionals had been over-zealous and the 'evidence' was unreliable. Specialist opinions (rather than agreed facts) were judged to have been given too much unquestioning credibility.

Similar issues have been raised again in the last few years about the extent to which sudden infant deaths may have had a deliberate rather than a natural cause and how much we can rely on the opinions of 'experts'. It is not always clear whether or not a child has been abused in many cases. The child may be very young or unable to give an account of what happened when no one else was present. Injuries may be inconclusive and capable of a variety of explanations. Abusers are often clever, manipulative and able to conceal what they have done, or are skilled at keeping professionals at arm's length. There can be a culture of denying everything, so that what can ultimately be proved is very limited. Yet we are still expected to detect abuse and even to try and predict it before it happens.

Despite our increased understanding, cases of avoidable child deaths have continued up to the present day (approximately two per week nationally). Most receive little publicity as they involve parents and carers, rather than the far smaller number that are about paedophiles, 'perverts' or strangers and which the media love so much. Inquiries into these cases, right up to Victoria Climbié, still suggest a failure of inter-agency communication as at least part of the reason why things went so badly wrong.

Most safeguarding decisions lie beyond the general expertise of teachers so it is vital that no action is taken by individual staff in schools without extensive consultation. Legislation has to strike a balance between the interests of all those involved, while putting primary emphasis on the welfare of the child. One agency or professional can only ever have a partial view of what may need to be done. This wider perspective was the specific intention of the Children Act 1989, which remains the legislative basis of current policy and practice.

Individual professionals also need to be clear that our own experiences may affect us in ways we might not always recognise. We were all children once. A professional may have been abused themselves or had bad experiences as a parent that might influence their thinking. Our personal value systems, or those of our school, may be severely tested by having to accept that such things go on where we are. But there is plenty of advice around which should help us to get it right as much as possible. It is essential that anyone with little previous direct experience of child protection becomes familiar with it. Young and disabled children are especially vulnerable but any child or young person may need action to protect them, so any teacher might need to act and at any time.

There are about 27,000 children on child protection registers in England and Wales (or, more correctly, with child protection plans), a fairly constant figure in recent years. But there is also a growing awareness of new kinds of abuse involving the Internet or someone outside the family in a position of trust. It is now recognised that much child abuse in the past was never acknowledged as such, especially abuse linked to domestic violence. Sexual abuse was routinely covered up, in families, institutions and organisations, and probably still is in many cases. The NSPCC estimate that only 1 in 4 cases is currently identified, even with the much higher profile now given to the issue. Abuse may still affect as many as 1 in 5 children.

Damaged adults are still carrying the scars of what happened to them years ago. They are far more likely than the population as a whole to be among those experiencing imprisonment, homelessness, unemployment, mental health problems and relationship breakdown as a result, especially if the abuse was not dealt with at the time. Child abuse is an enemy of social inclusion, as well as of personal well-being.

Guidance

The government issues guidance to all agencies every few years, constantly updating it in the light of experience. *Working Together to Safeguard Children* and *The Framework for the Assessment of Children in Need and their Families* were originally published in 1999 and 2000 respectively. These revised all previous advice on the basis of new research into what had been happening over the previous two decades. Together they widened the focus of the agencies that deal with children and their families to ensure that effective measures to safeguard children should not be seen in isolation from a wider range of support services intended to meet their needs.

As outlined in Chapter 1, the emphasis now lies in the development of comprehensive family support services, and we are trying to move away from being only 'incident-driven'. But the need to deal with cases of acute risk must always continue alongside any more supportive approach. No matter how good our emphasis on prevention, some children will always be killed, injured, neglected or otherwise abused by their parents, carers and others. Many of them will never have come to the attention of agencies before. Abuse does not happen only in 'problem' families but across all classes, cultures and communities. All workers with children therefore need to be constantly vigilant.

WORKING TOGETHER TO SAFEGUARD CHILDREN

The 2006 edition states that:

Schools (including independent schools and non-maintained special schools) and Further Education (FE) institutions should give effect to their duty to safeguard and promote the welfare of pupils . . . by

- Creating and maintaining a safe learning environment for children and young people; and,

- Identifying where there are child welfare concerns and taking action to address them, in partnership with other organisations where appropriate.

. . .

Education staff have a crucial role to play in helping to identify welfare concerns, and indicators of possible abuse or neglect at an early stage: referring those concerns to the appropriate organisation, normally social services colleagues, contributing to the assessment of a child's needs and where appropriate to ongoing action to meet those needs. (paras. 2.121 and 2.123)

In the light of the death of Lauren Wright in May 2000 and the following formal Inquiry, section 175 of the Education Act 2002 came into force on 1 June 2004. This requires all schools, governors, FE colleges and local authorities to carry out their functions in a way that 'safeguards and promotes' the welfare of children. Staff and managers in all schools must 'have regard' to the statutory Guidance, *Safeguarding Children and Safer Recruitment in Education* (2006). This replaced the previous Circular 0027/2004 and is essential reading. Copies can be downloaded or ordered from http://www.teachernet.gov.uk/ and www.dfes.gov.uk/safeguardingchildren/.

As noted in Chapter 1, further significant changes to the whole inter-agency child protection and child welfare system are being introduced in response to the death of Victoria Climbié, the subsequent Laming Report, the Green Paper *Every Child Matters* and the Children Act 2004. The DfES now carries overall responsibility for all children's services, including social work, not just education. This change is increasingly reflected at local authority level in new working relationships as more multi-disciplinary Children's Services Authorities are emerging, rather than maintaining the previous distinction between education, health and social care professionals.

Local Safeguarding Children Boards

Key to this process, and to the delivery of the specific outcomes about children being healthy and safe, is the creation of Local Safeguarding Children Boards (LSCB) to replace the previous Area Child Protection Committees (ACPC). These have been fully in place since April 2006. They are more strategic bodies with wider responsibilities, intended to ensure effective practice and hold agencies to account rather more than used to be the case. There will also be greater use of shared children's data and agreed thresholds of concern in order to facilitate more effective inter-agency working through new local Multi-Agency Support Teams. These other key local developments for supporting children and families, and the revised inter-agency procedures that will now be in place, should all be seen alongside the guidance specifically aimed at education.

There is now a general trend towards using the word 'safeguarding' rather than 'protecting'. While the two are sometimes used interchangeably, safeguarding is intended to convey a broader concept that includes prevention and addressing issues that put children's welfare at risk beyond the strict definitions of 'abuse' as outlined below. In a school context, for example, safeguarding would include measures to combat bullying and safe staff recruitment and appointment procedures (in the light of Ian Huntley and Soham). It could also include ensuring the safety of children on trips and when using the school's facilities outside school hours. LSCBs will also have an interest in the welfare of particular groups such as privately fostered children and will be required to review all unexpected child deaths, not just those identified as abuse.

However, it is extremely important not to lose sight of the needs of individual children for protection from harm when required. As has been reiterated by the Inquiry into a serious case of neglect in Sheffield reported by their ACPC in December 2005, the needs of the individual child must remain the focus. In this case, agencies became far too tolerant of poor standards of care that were putting the children at risk. There is a new emphasis on:

- ensuring that professionals are competent in carrying out their duties and improving the standard of the safeguarding service;
- reinforcing the duty to take the necessary steps to protect children and young people when required;
- accepting personal responsibility for acting on information that may be known to you alone; and
- corporate ownership of the desired outcomes, not a 'culture of referral' that seeks to transfer responsibility on to someone else. This is as true for educational professionals as for anyone else, including both teaching and non-teaching staff and in any setting.

Arrangements in schools

Workers in individual agencies must also be fully aware of where they fit within local procedures that will define the limits of their role. To help all staff in direct contact with children to get this right, there must be a designated senior person in every school, and a written child protection policy which should be made known to parents. (The local authority may issue schools with a 'model'.) These arrangements should ensure that all staff have the information and procedures that they need. No one should ever make a child protection decision without following an agreed procedure.

The designated person should ensure that child protection is included in programmes of induction; that support and advice is available and that everyone is familiar with the school's policy. They may also make use of local inter-agency procedures, written guidance from education lead officers and the government booklet *What to do if You are Worried a Child is being Abused* (DoH 2006), or a local equivalent. School-based INSET may also be available and all teachers are expected to have received training at least every three years. Awareness of these issues could all be the subject of enquiry as part of an inspection. What follows below provides a basic overview but is no substitute for being fully familiar with the local inter-agency procedures.

Child protection practice in schools

Confidentiality and information-sharing

It is very important that all those involved in concerns about the care of children should share the same understanding of confidentiality and when it should be broken. Children are not protected if nobody shares what they know. Research and experience have shown repeatedly that keeping children safe from harm requires professionals and others to talk to each other. The Children Act 2004 creates a new legal framework within which shared databases can be developed that can highlight the concerns that may have been expressed by a range of professionals and agencies, though progress has so far been quite slow except in those areas given additional resources as 'pilots'.

All education settings should have a written statement of confidentiality making clear the duty to share information with other agencies such as social services and the police in certain circumstances. This should be published in any information given to pupils and parents when they first come into contact with the establishment. In light of the Freedom of Information Act 2000, this statement could be included with the school's child protection policy so that parents are fully aware of it. This will help to set any action taken into context and make it less likely that parents will react entirely negatively if staff members feel they need to act on any concern. Child protection cannot be done anonymously or in secret.

In matters concerning child protection, confidentiality means that any conversation or information given will be treated in complete privacy and will not be shared indiscriminately with others. Gossip should, of course, be avoided. However, in order to protect the best interests of a child or young person, the information may be shared with other professionals to enable action to be taken by others. No one should ever make a promise to a child that they will keep child protection concerns a secret. They must be told that the information has to be shared in order to protect them. If you don't tell someone else, you can't do anything yourself to stop the abuse. The child or young person has to be helped to understand that.

Whenever information gathered at school is passed on, like an injury that is seen there or something a child says that causes concern, the action being taken should also be explained to them (if he/she is old enough). It may reassure them to know that only people outside the school will be told. Also, and this is sometimes difficult, parents should be told of the action being taken unless, in the professional's judgement, it may put the child at increased risk of harm to do so. Whether or not the parent should be made aware of the referral immediately, and if not, why not, will normally be raised by the designated person in the school as part of the referral process. This decision should not be left to the person who first noticed the injury or other clue to abuse.

DEFINITIONS

Section 47 of the Children Act 1989 contains the duty that where a local authority:

(a) is informed that a child who lives, or is found, in their area, is the subject of an emergency protection order, or is in police protection, or

(b) has reasonable cause to suspect that a child who lives, or is found in their area is suffering, or is likely to suffer, significant harm,

the authority shall make, or cause to be made, such enquires as it considers necessary to enable it to decide whether it should take action to safeguard or promote the child's welfare.

The concept of 'significant harm' was introduced in the Children Act 1989 as the threshold that justifies compulsory intervention in family life in the best interests of children. There are no absolute criteria on which to rely when judging what constitutes significant harm. A court may only make a care order or a supervision order in respect of a child if it is satisfied that:

the child is suffering, or is likely to suffer, significant harm; and that the harm, or likelihood of harm is attributable to lack of adequate parental care or control (s. 31).

'Harm' means ill treatment or the impairment of health or development; 'development' means physical, intellectual, emotional, social or behavioural development; 'health' means physical or mental health; 'ill treatment' includes sexual abuse and forms of ill treatment which are not physical.

Where the question of whether harm suffered by a child is significant turns on the child's health and development, his health or development shall be compared with that which could reasonably be expected of a similar child (s. 31(10)).

The rather complex legal definitions mean that there may not be immediate agreement among professionals about whether or not the threshold for compulsory intervention to protect a child has been reached. As far as practicable, all those who work with children need to have a common sense of what may constitute a child protection issue or what level of concern justifies sharing information with the social services and police under child protection procedures. Only they are empowered to establish more fully the level of risk to the child, following further enquiries.

To help those, like teachers, whose main task is to make referrals, not to carry out the investigations themselves, *Working Together* contains some practical guidance that will normally be repeated in local LSCB procedures. Advice can also be found in the DfES Guidance (2006).

Categories of abuse: signs and symptoms

Working Together (2006) definitions are best quoted in full as they are common to all practice across the country:

> Somebody may abuse or neglect a child by inflicting harm, or by failing to act to prevent harm. Children may be abused in a family or in an institutional or community setting by those known to them or, more rarely by a stranger. They may be abused by an adult or adults or another child or children (para. 1.29).

Physical abuse may involve hitting, shaking, throwing, poisoning, burning or scalding, drowning, suffocating or otherwise causing physical harm to a child. Physical harm may also be caused when a parent or carer fabricates the symptoms of, or deliberately induces illness in a child (1.30).

POSSIBLE SIGNS OF PHYSICAL ABUSE

- Unexplained injuries, bites, bruises or burns, particularly if they are recurrent
- Improbable excuses given to explain injuries
- Refusal to discuss the causes of injuries
- Untreated injuries
- Disclosure of punishment which appears excessive
- Withdrawal from physical contact/aggressive behaviour
- Arms and legs kept covered in hot weather (excluding for reasons of cultural dress)
- Fear of returning home
- Fear of medical help
- Self-destructive tendency
- Running away

Emotional abuse is the persistent emotional ill-treatment of a child such as to cause severe and persistent adverse effects on the child's emotional development. It may involve conveying to children that they are worthless or unloved, inadequate, or valued only insofar as they meet the needs of another person. It may feature age or developmentally inappropriate expectations being imposed on children. These may include interactions that are beyond the child's developmental capability, as well as overprotection and limitation of exploring and learning, or preventing the child participating in normal social interaction. It may involve seeing or hearing the ill-treatment of another. It may involve serious bullying, causing children frequently to feel frightened or in danger, or the exploitation or corruption of children. Some level of emotional abuse is involved in all types of ill-treatment of a child, though it may occur alone (1.31).

POSSIBLE SIGNS OF EMOTIONAL ABUSE

- Physical, mental or emotional/developmental lag
- Domestic violence
- Disclosure of punishment which appears excessive
- Over-reaction to making mistakes or fear of punishment
- Continual self-deprecation
- Sudden speech disorders
- Fear of new situations
- Inappropriate responses to painful situations
- Neurotic behaviours
- Self-harm
- Fear of parents being contacted
- Extremes of passivity or aggression
- Drug or solvent abuse
- Running away
- Compulsive stealing, scavenging

Sexual abuse involves forcing or enticing a child or young person to take part in sexual activities, including prostitution, whether or not the child is aware of what is happening. The activities may involve physical contact, including penetrative or non-penetrative acts. They may include non-contact activities, such as involving children in looking at, or in the production of pornographic material or watching sexual activities, or encouraging children to behave in sexually inappropriate ways (1.32).

POSSIBLE SIGNS OF SEXUAL ABUSE

- Sudden changes in performance or behaviour at school
- Displays of affection in a sexual way which is inappropriate to age
- Alleged promiscuity
- Tendency to cry easily

- Regression to younger behaviour such as thumbsucking, playing with discarded toys, acting like a baby
- Tendency to cling or need reassurance
- Distrust of familiar adult, or anxiety about being left with a relative, babysitter, lodger, etc.
- Unexplained gifts of money
- Depression and withdrawal
- Apparent secrecy about social activities or the identity of 'special friends'
- Wetting or soiling, day and night
- Sleep disturbances or nightmares
- Chronic illness, especially throat infections and sexually transmitted diseases
- Anorexia or bulimia
- Unacknowledged pregnancy
- Fear of undressing, e.g. for sport
- Phobias or panic attacks

Neglect is the persistent failure to meet a child's basic physical and or psychological needs, likely to result in the serious impairment of the child's health or development. It may involve a parent or carer failing to provide adequate food, shelter and clothing, failing to protect a child from physical harm or danger, or the failure to ensure access to appropriate medical care or treatment. It may also include neglect of, or unresponsiveness to, a child's basic emotional needs (1.33).

POSSIBLE SIGNS OF NEGLECT

- Constant hunger
- Poor personal hygiene
- Constant tiredness
- Poor state of clothing
- Frequent lateness or non-attendance at school
- Untreated medical problems or unmet special needs
- Low self-esteem
- Neurotic behaviour
- Poor social relationships
- Running away
- Compulsive stealing or scavenging

Responding to concerns

Serious concerns about the welfare of children and young people, actual disclosures of possible abuse and observations of behaviour or injuries that appear suspicious, should be reported immediately within local procedures. Of course we do not always spot the signs of abuse. The child or parent may actively try to prevent us doing so. None of these indicators prove it must be abuse. But all education staff share the responsibility for ensuring that, as far as reasonably possible, concerns are brought to the attention of the responsible person/agency in order that they may be investigated further.

Central education staff who visit different schools and educational settings, such as educational psychologists and other support staff working with children with SEN, should acquaint themselves with the school's child protection policy and procedures and the identity of the designated person for each establishment. Normally a referral for a child in that school should only be made in consultation with the designated person (unless it is out of hours, an emergency or a school holiday).

The conduct of front-line staff can significantly influence the outcome of subsequent court proceedings, so all teaching and non-teaching staff must follow strict guidelines concerning the collection of evidence.

COLLECTING EVIDENCE

- Anyone hearing a disclosure of abuse must take care not to ask the child leading questions or put ideas into his/her mind about what may have happened. It must be their story.

- You should listen carefully and say as little as possible beyond supporting the child and making it clear that you are listening.

- Do not be drawn into conducting an investigation yourself or trying to find out what 'really' happened.

- Written records should be kept of all concerns and particularly of occasions when a child discloses incidents that may be regarded as abuse.

- Do not require the child to make any form of 'statement' to school staff or take any photographs. (If the child has visible injuries, it is essential to refer them immediately so that others can gather the necessary evidence while they are still visible.) Drawings such as outline body maps are acceptable as an interim record.

- Date and sign all records when completed but never ask the child to sign anything.

- Report concerns immediately to the designated person whose responsibility it is to decide what action should be taken.

- If unsure, take advice.

More generally, all education staff, teachers, local authority officers, classroom assistants, helpers and parent volunteers also need to be aware of the way in which their actions may be perceived. We must be careful not to act in any ways that leave ourselves, or any child, at risk of allegations of abuse. Always seek advice and information about good practice, particularly in relation to high risk areas such as:

- dealing with aggression and violence
- the use of legitimate force or restraint
- individual work with children and young people, especially in unsupervised settings or in their homes
- social contact with pupils outside school
- e-mail and text-messaging
- any situation that involves the delivery of personal or intimate care.

Disabled children

It is widely recognised that the safeguarding process does not always serve the best interests of children with special educational needs and disabilities as well as it should, despite their known increased vulnerability. Where children have communication difficulties they may not be considered able to give witness testimony in a way that can satisfy the rigorous requirements of an adversarial court system. It may not always be possible to use the legal system to bring about convictions as may happen for other children. This will be especially true if there is little or no corroborating or independent forensic evidence to support the child's version of events. Abusers will be well aware of these limitations and may take every opportunity to exploit them. However, these obstacles should never be allowed to mean that the child protection system is not available to them or that referrals should not be made on their behalf as for any other child or young person.

Post-abuse support

It can be difficult for school staff to know how much they should talk to the pupil about any incident for some time afterwards, especially if court proceedings are pending. There can be lengthy delays before a serious case may come to court. In the meantime, continuing to engage the child in education may be a considerable challenge, especially if they are traumatised or still coping with the effects of the disruption caused by their disclosure. It is not true that no one should ever mention the subject for fear of causing the child further distress or contaminating their possible future evidence. Normal pastoral care to support the child will still be appropriate.

It is important to make sure that any specific counselling or therapeutic work has been agreed by the child's social worker and, if necessary, by the court. There is the possibility that a defence case might suggest that the child has been influenced by subsequent work undertaken with professionals to give a version of events which is what they think others want to hear, rather than being an accurate account of what actually happened, perhaps many months before. School staff should not make such arrangements themselves without wider consultation first.

The inter-agency safeguarding process

Initial investigation

Once the referral has been made, what happens next? There is a widespread misunderstanding, often perpetuated by some elements of the media, that social workers and police officers frequently arrive unannounced on people's doorsteps at six o'clock in the morning, blue lights flashing. They then drag people's children away from them, kicking and screaming, to place them presumably with people who will then abuse them while in their care!

Of course there are times when secrecy is necessary in order to ensure that evidence is not destroyed and that children are not exposed to even greater danger. I was once involved in a case where a child reported activities at their home which included other children being brought to the house to be sexually abused, the video of which was then sold on to their parents. Extreme criminal behaviour of this kind obviously requires a carefully managed covert response. Similar caution and an element of surprise may be needed in response to concerns about Internet child pornography or if more than one abuser may be involved.

But most of the time child protection isn't like that and referrals are normally dealt with in an entirely different way. For most children, no matter how great the problems they are experiencing, their home is their home and their family is their family. It will rarely be in their best interests to risk destroying all that may be positive in the attempt to deal with what is wrong. Children often love the person who is harming them, and do not want to be moved away from their siblings, friends and school as if they were somehow the source of the problem themselves. Social workers are skilled in managing these issues on a daily basis. Indeed it may sometimes seem that they are trying too hard to keep the family together. But they have a duty to do so, unless the child's best interests suggest otherwise or in situations of extreme danger.

Acting on a referral usually involves:

- An initial response by the social work duty team to determine the current level of risk to the child. This may mean them having to take immediate action, before the child can go home from school, so the earlier in the day such referrals are made the better. But it may be that the risk will not occur until they next visit their grandparents or in some other less acute situation, so more time may elapse before a response is required.

- A discussion between the social worker and the police. This should ideally be in the form of a strategy meeting that also involves the referrer, but in an emergency it is more likely to be just over the phone or in the car on the way to the home visit. This initial meeting is to determine what each agency's involvement might need to be, especially if any criminal offences may be involved or if there is a need for an individual to be arrested. It will also consider whether the children need to be removed under the emergency powers that only the police (not social workers) have available for an immediate response.

- Contacting all other agencies that may know the child to see whether or not they have any information that might suggest either an increased or decreased risk, alongside the information received from the referrer. This may be the first that a school knows about a case that has begun elsewhere. It is important that all known facts, about both children and parents, are shared if requested. This is part of the statutory duty.

- Actually seeing the child and arranging a medical examination by a specialist paediatrician if there is an urgent need for treatment or if expert testimony may be required. This would include, for example, a judgement about the possible cause of any injury or for the gathering of forensic material which may be essential for a future prosecution. This is one reason why a referral has to be made immediately if the child has a suspicious injury. By tomorrow it may not be possible even for an expert to determine its likely cause.

- Interviewing the child on video by specialist police officers and social workers if they have a story to tell that can help to establish exactly what has happened. This video, as well as giving the child an early opportunity to tell their story in their own words, also provides 'evidence in chief' for future use in either criminal or care proceedings. These interviews operate according to strict Home Office guidelines about the kinds of questions that can be asked in order to avoid contaminating the child's potential evidence.

- An assessment of current and longer-term risk by the social worker and their manager in order to make a decision about what should happen next and over how long a time. This whole process may be done in a day, or over several days or weeks, depending on the child's circumstances and the nature of the concern.

Following this initial response, the case may be closed because it has been dealt with. For example, advice may be given to parents about improved parenting, the family could be referred elsewhere, or the concern is found to be unjustified. Such an outcome would not mean that the referral was inappropriate. The assessment to establish that the child is safe could not have taken place without it. But social workers will usually prefer to deal with low-level concerns in low-level ways. Serious or continuing concerns that suggest the child remains at risk of significant harm should not, however, be dealt with so quickly. Referrers may need to follow up their original referral by contacting a more senior manager if they remain concerned for the child's welfare and it appears that nothing effective has happened in response. That is part of everyone's responsibility.

Child Protection Conferences

Even quite serious cases may not need any further agency involvement, if for example, criminal proceedings are under way and the child is now safe. But if unresolved issues of risk remain, an initial Child Protection Conference is called. This is in order to:

- pool information about a child and their family,
- assess the level of known risk to this child and any other child in the family, and
- decide whether there are sufficient grounds for drawing up a multi-agency Child Protection Plan. (This was formerly described as placing the child on the Child Protection Register.)

The emphasis has moved away from seeing registration as the end product in order to make it clear that it is the agreed actions that will be undertaken under the Plan that actually protect the child, not their admission to a list. There will still need to be a local way for practitioners to check whether a child currently has a Plan – effectively creating the need for a register by any other name. However, this list may now be integrated within general child information systems rather than as a stand-alone 'register' as before.

Normally, both the person who raised the concern and the school's designated person would be expected to attend the initial conference. Headteachers are required to provide the necessary cover to enable key people to be at the meeting. The school will also need to be represented at those conferences about cases where staff have information to share, even if the referral has come from elsewhere. Attendance should be seen as an absolute priority if you are invited, as conferences cannot take place without a sufficient range of agencies present. They inevitably happen at fairly short notice and may be lengthy.

Other education officers, such as education welfare officers or educational psychologists may also be invited, but only if they also have personal knowledge of the child/family. Everyone who attends will then be responsible for sharing in a corporate decision about whether the continuing level of risk justifies a Plan. If so, this decision will be reviewed after three and then six months. Attendance at these future conferences is just as important as attendance at the first one.

A REPORT FOR A CHILD PROTECTION CONFERENCE

What information will be needed from the school's representative? Local procedures may give further guidance but it is important to contribute information covering issues such as:

- educational progress in comparison with peers

- general health and emotional well-being

- the child's ability to relate to peers and staff

- attendance record

- parent/carer information (e.g. contact with school)

- any injuries seen or information given by child which has caused concerns

- the child's view of themselves and their family

Such information should be factual, balanced, fair and accurate and free of personal opinions and judgements, drawing attention to strengths within the family as well as weaknesses and risks. The report will be made available to parents, and if appropriate, to the child. If needed, an opportunity should also exist to share information without the parent present (if they are the alleged perpetrator), usually at the request of the police.

Core group meetings and the Child Protection Plan

If a Plan is necessary, action will be required immediately after the conference. This was always the essential element in the procedure, not just adding the child's name to a list: the need to act has now been made more explicit. The designated person will need to take responsibility for ensuring that key school staff in contact with the child or young person are aware of their new status. They need to understand the implications of the Plan or other recommendations that may affect their actions (e.g. immediately reporting any unexplained absences or sudden changes in the child's behaviour, attitude or circumstances). The keyworker (a social worker) must be kept informed of any developments. The designated person will also need to ensure that minutes are securely stored and available for future reference. This includes passing records on in confidence to any subsequent school.

The core group is a small group of members of the initial conference. They will:

- devise the Child Protection Plan,
- monitor the day-to-day progress of the case,
- complete the Core Assessment of the child's needs (if this has not happened already), and
- review any on-going risks to the child's safety and welfare.

Crucially, this process also has to consider what action will have to be taken, including court proceedings, if the child continues to be at risk of significant harm or if progress in safeguarding their welfare is not being made. Even the Plan and the Assessment are only steps on the road to promoting the child's welfare; if that is not being achieved, other steps will be needed as well.

Core group meetings are likely to take place quite frequently, particularly in the early stages of the Plan, maybe fortnightly or monthly. Headteachers must ensure that staff are given the time to attend that is required. (This may even have to be in a school holiday.) The group is a sub-committee of the original Conference and all decisions must be ratified by the Conference or subsequent reviews. The importance of attending reviews and core groups cannot be over-emphasised. This will inform the planning process in keeping the child safe, enable information to be shared and ensure that the school remains fully informed of their current circumstances.

A Child Protection Plan should not last forever and, if things have improved, a subsequent review conference can 'de-register' the child again. This should not lead to the family then losing all the support that has been previously available. But once it has been established that the risk to the child has been diminished, this support should be offered in other, less invasive, ways that enable parents to make decisions without the need for more supervised arrangements (see Chapter 1).

Older children and young people

Much of the most urgent child protection work relates to very young, and therefore very vulnerable children and babies, most of which is never seen by school staff. The issues can be somewhat more complex with older young people but the system is intended to provide protection for those up to 18. (Other procedures should also be in place to protect vulnerable young adults, e.g. in special schools.) However, things often have to be done differently when the young person is an active partner in determining their own level of risk. They may be engaging in risky sexual behaviour, self-harming or abusing substances. They may themselves pose a significant risk to other children, either physically or sexually, at school and in the community. This makes their needs a wider safeguarding issue, not just a disciplinary matter for the staff to deal with alone.

In general, any actual or potential sexual activity involving a child under 13 and another person, adult or child, should always be considered a child protection issue in the first instance. Advice must be sought from specialist professionals before deciding whether to keep the information confidential. This is potentially an offence of 'statutory rape' as a child of this age cannot give informed consent. (This requirement need not, of course, include perfectly normal behaviours where very young children are simply curious about their own or other children's bodies.)

There is more discretion between 13 and 16. There is no automatic obligation on school staff to inform parents or agencies if the activity is said to be non-coercive and is within conventional boundaries between those of similar ages. However, no one should ever forget Ian Huntley and his serial abuse of younger girls, allegedly as their 'boyfriend'. Earlier action might have saved lives later. 'Abuse' still needs to be recognised as such and referred. Again, seek advice if you are unsure.

Gaining the young person's consent to any intervention will be crucial in the longer term, but, if the threshold of the risk of 'significant harm' is met, child protection concerns should still be raised even if the young person is not initially co-operative. Many behaviours present as self-induced but may also be a response to physical, emotional or sexual exploitation. It is essential in such situations still to see such a child as a child 'in need', entitled to protection, and not only as the source of their own difficulties and therefore somehow to blame for them.

Allegations against staff

This is an area of considerable concern to teachers, not least because some children, especially those who are disaffected and experiencing social exclusion, may occasionally make allegations that have no basis. They are, after all children, who might be expected to behave in a childish way now and again! Adults may have often been unfair with them too and this may be one way of trying to get even. However, even if some cases have been mishandled, and some certainly are, 'professional abuse' is a reality, not wholly a myth and we need to be aware of it. School is an ideal to place to be if your intentions towards children are inappropriate. The danger is that our perceptions about these incidents may cloud our judgement on all other abuse issues as well.

Sometimes children or parents may seek to exploit a situation where there is no real basis for concern. Many other situations arise because of misunderstandings or misinterpretations. But the assessment that there is no cause for concern in a particular case should not be made by a headteacher alone without any consultation with others in the local authority who will have more specialist knowledge. All allegations with any substance at all need to be properly and independently investigated, outside the school.

ALLEGATIONS: DEFINITIONS

Working Together to Safeguard Children (2006) indicates that there are three circumstances in which child protection procedures must be invoked:

The framework for managing cases set out in this guidance . . . should be used in respect of all cases in which it is alleged that a person who works with children has:

- behaved in a way that has harmed a child or may have harmed a child; or
- possibly committed a criminal offence against or related to a child; or
- behaved towards a child or children in a way that indicates s/he is unsuitable to work with children. (Appendix 5, para. 1)

The fairly wide definition in the guidance covers a range of incidents where a child may have been harmed by an adult or it is alleged that they have been. Parents and children have the right to make complaints and it is important not to send a signal that any complaint will be seen automatically as malicious or unfounded. There is always a danger that otherwise this will deter the child who has a genuine concern that someone in a position of trust is acting inappropriately towards them. We must be very careful not to suggest that such things cannot possibly happen here, should not be talked about and that the child will get into trouble if they do. The abuser may well be doing that already.

Trivial allegations should be quickly identified and no further action may need to be taken once they have been investigated. A strategy meeting may not even be needed if the facts are clear, but those responsible for calling them must make that decision, not the school. Only those concerns that are 'demonstrably false' (i.e. with no basis in fact: not just a difference of opinion about something that did actually happen) need not be reported under local inter-agency procedures. As with any child protection investigation, only the police and social workers have the necessary powers to establish the facts. An 'investigation' by a headteacher has no validity if what is being investigated is a possible criminal offence, and this may leave everyone, including the teacher, feeling that the matter has never been properly concluded. This uncertainty is in no one's interests.

Concerns that reach the inter-agency process may still lie permanently on a professional's record, even if found to be untrue or unsubstantiated. The police may therefore reveal them during a subsequent Criminal Records Bureau check as 'soft' information. Understandably this is a worry for teachers. Since the Soham murders it is more likely that a wider range of information will now be disclosed, as sometimes this will still be relevant in deciding whether someone is suitable to work with children, even if there have been no offences proven. However, the police will not always see the need to disclose it and employers are also becoming more adept at determining what such information means. Many people who work with children and young people, especially those who are challenging, including residential care workers, police officers and others are in such a position, not just teachers.

If the facts indicate that there is a real risk to children or that a criminal offence which would result in disqualification from teaching may have occurred, any disciplinary procedure will have to be integrated with both police investigations and wider enquiries into child protection concerns, for example, within the individual's own family. This will be managed through a strategy meeting to which the headteacher or chair of governors should always be routinely invited as the person's immediate employer. There should be a minimum of intervention before this meeting has taken place to co-ordinate the response.

If suspension is required, that is a matter for the employer alone, though it is usually wise to act on any advice from the police or social worker. Unfortunately many of the more complex cases can take a considerable time to resolve but every local authority should now have an allegations manager whose job it is to oversee such enquiries and ensure as speedy a resolution as possible.

Staff recruitment

Recruitment and selection procedures have become much more thorough since the Bichard Inquiry into how Ian Huntley was appointed as a school caretaker, given his previous history of inappropriate sexual activity with under-age girls. Candidates for all posts that involve contact with children must expect to produce evidence of their qualifications and specific references that relate to the kind of post for which they are applying, not open references marked 'To whom it may concern'. Potential employers should speak directly to referees about the requirements of the particular job involved and CRB checks must be completed before the individual starts work. In due course regular checks are expected to become routine for all of us, not just when we change employers.

There has been a steep learning curve for some of those in education as the professional standards previously expected in social care appointments are now being applied across all of children's services. This happened in most residential schools and children's homes some years ago as result of the raised standards of the Children Act 1989. It is interesting that day schools have not always expected the same high standards of their staff that are applicable elsewhere.

It is especially important to discuss the boundaries of appropriate conduct with newly qualified staff who may not have had much previous opportunity to do so. Similarly there may be risks to be addressed with more experienced staff who may not yet have accepted the kind of scrutiny and accountability that now has to be in place. This is all intended to deter the person who may pose a risk. For those who do not, it may be irksome at times but all this has to be seen as a necessary precaution, in children's best interests and, ultimately, in our own as well.

Conclusion

No one wants to have to deal with a child protection issue and you may go for years without being in that position. If policies and procedures are in place, and followed as they should be, it should be less stressful when the time comes than if you are left to sort it for yourself. Things often do not turn out as well as we might have hoped; family secrets once uncovered can have a devastating impact in both the short and the long term. Confidence among teachers in how other professionals will deal with their concerns is often low. Those in other agencies often feel the same about teachers' capacity to make appropriate referrals as they should. There is a constant need for dialogue and joint training in order to establish good working practices.

We have to get past such mutual suspicion if we are to make a difference in children's lives as the social inclusion agenda requires. Here in particular, professionals need to trust each other and learn to work together. If we cannot, it can only be worse for the children and young people we are supposed to be protecting. The historically poor outcomes of those children have been a blight on young lives that we must always seek to avoid wherever humanly possible.

Children at risk of missing education

I went to school like everyone else when I was a kid. Things were fine till I went into care. It wasn't my fault mum couldn't cope. I wanted to stay with her but they said she couldn't look after us. We used to go and see her in the hospital at first but then she said she didn't want to see us any more. The first foster home was alright; they used to take me to the sea at weekends. But I didn't get on at the second one and I had to move three times that year. After mum died I just lost interest in school, what with all the changes. When I was in Tower Court no-one went to school much. It was great – we just used to muck about all day. I suppose I should have got some exams but it's too late now. I'll get by.

Missing out

What is currently going on in schools can sometimes appear to be the sole focus of educational thinking. This risks a lack of interest in those who have always been the most vulnerable group of children in our society – those who are not participating in education at all: those who have no school to go to and possibly no other provision either. Transferring greater responsibilities to schools, either individually or in partnerships, assumes that all children are registered pupils somewhere. But many are not. Victoria Climbié was a child like this; she was never part of the school system. So clearly this is a vital issue that cannot be ignored if our intention is to make things better for those who are truly on the margins.

Being known to a school and on their registers is a valuable protection that is not available if we don't even know that the child or young person exists. They may be absent a lot, or even excluded, but we still know about them and where they are. We will at least be able to try and meet their needs, if in other ways. The child who doesn't appear on the database is denied all that, so this is both a safeguarding and an educational duty that must be given the highest priority.

These children may also be missing out on much more than education. They may be living in an entirely separate counter-culture that does nothing to promote social inclusion or to open up choices and opportunities for them within the wider society. In particular, their parents may not be acting in what is ultimately their children's best interests. They may even pose a direct threat to them, without the usual monitoring offered by regular engagement with mainstream services.

The DfES now expects robust multi-agency systems to be in place to ensure that such children can be identified, tracked and crucially, have their need for education met. Just knowing who they are is not enough. Authorities that do not deliver on these key measures may even face 'naming and shaming'. This is a significant task that is probably still not being fully achieved in many areas, especially if the local community is characterised by a transient population with more than its fair share of marginalised groups. Identifying them is hard enough but that is only the means, not the end. What matters is that we then make services available and raise their attainment. Education professionals cannot do this on their own, but the success of the whole 'Every Child Matters' agenda is at stake here.

WHO ARE WE TALKING ABOUT?

All agencies that work with children have a shared responsibility:

- the health visitor who is concerned that the child they see at home in the daytime isn't in school and doesn't seem to have one to go to;
- the police officer who apprehends a young person committing an offence in school time and who says he hasn't been to school for months;
- the worker from a voluntary agency who is providing support to an elderly, disabled or chronically ill person where a child appears to be a regular daytime carer.

Add to these:

- the children of asylum–seekers and refugees, some of whom may be here illegally;
- recent arrivals in the area;
- children whose parents are deliberately avoiding school;
- young offenders deemed too dangerous to be in school;
- those living away from their parents and families;
- those who are homeless, pregnant or members of communities that travel;
- those who have been excluded long term, formally or informally.

One difficulty is that, by definition, we do not know how many such children there are. There are no lists of children that are not on the list! The DfES have suggested at least 10,000 at any one time and many more who are at risk of being lost. That is probably an under-estimate, and only includes those towards the top of the age range. Local authorities do not necessarily know about everyone who is living in their area. The new child index planned under the Children Act 2004 will make a significant difference, but we are not there yet and many of those about whom there is most concern will still not be on it. While there is a legal requirement to register every child at birth we cannot always keep track of them thereafter.

No one knows how many children do not feature in official statistics, either because their parents do not wish them to or because the family are recent arrivals in an area and there is no obligation on them to inform anyone that they are there. Not everyone even registers with a doctor and, crucially, there is no duty to tell anyone if you choose to educate your children at home, only if you are withdrawing them from a school to do so. If the child has never been to a school, we may never know about them. It is not uncommon for local authorities to come across children and young people who have never attended a school or who have disappeared after primary school and entirely dropped out of education as a result.

The only approach to addressing this situation is through sharing information wherever possible and making sure that no one agency acts in a way that compromises the role of another. Schools and other agencies have not always been active partners in local arrangements. But we are all now required to ensure that suitable safeguards are in place both to minimise the risk of losing touch with children and to ensure that those who do come to light have access to provision without difficulty. Both of these duties will be significant challenges. The parents, children and young people concerned may well be among those whose life experiences have taught them that adults in general, and agencies in particular, let you down when you need them. Just telling them that we know best is not likely to take us very far.

> ## DFES GUIDANCE FOR SCHOOLS
>
> The current key DfES document is *Identifying and Maintaining Contact with Children Missing, or at Risk of Going Missing, from Education* (0225/2004). (A revised version, if substantially the same, is expected following the introduction of the new statutory duty proposed in the Education and Inspections Act 2006.) Few frontline practitioners will be familiar with it but your local authority should have developed a protocol for working arrangements in the light of it. It provides a useful overview of the general principles, before looking in more detail at some the specific groups known to be at greatest risk. There will be a designated officer in the Education/Children's Service with responsibility for Children Missing Education (CME) and perhaps even a specialist team for missing children in some areas. But the issues reach down to every school and every person who may be aware of a child who appears not to be engaging in education. The duty to do something about it clearly lies with them to act on what they know, at least in the first instance.

Off-registration procedures

The most likely role of a school is making sure that correct procedures are followed if a child goes missing, i.e. stops attending and appears to be no longer at the address where they were living previously. Where children are just absent, other procedures need to be followed, but if they are absent and 'missing' schools need to do rather more. It will almost certainly be the role of the education welfare officer (EWO) to follow up such children and try to establish what has happened. Pupils should not be off-registered until such enquiries have been completed.

Unilateral action to remove a child from the Admission Register prematurely will almost certainly complicate things. This will mean having to carry the absences, at least in the short-term, until more information has been obtained. If off-registration is appropriate it can usually be backdated to the pupil's last attendance. Along with the avoidance of unofficial exclusions as outlined in Chapter 3, good practice here will almost certainly ensure that children do not end up out of school unnecessarily. Once off a register it can be very difficult for the child to get back on again, at that school or anywhere else. For statemented pupils, of course, there must be full consultation with the local authority before any action is taken that changes the provision that has already been agreed with the parents. The registration regulations specifically make it clear that this decision does not lie with the headteacher alone.

LOST PUPILS DATABASE AND SCHOOL2SCHOOL

If a pupil is legally off-registered, and the current school does not know where they have gone after reasonable enquiry, use should be made of the Lost Pupils Database (LPD) within School2School (S2S). (For further advice see http://www.teachernet.gov.uk/s2s/) Schools now routinely transfer information electronically when children change provision, using the Common Transfer File (CTF). Making such information available is a legal requirement under the Education Pupil Information) (England) Regulations 2000.

S2S provides a facility for secure messaging that can be used for targeted emails about specific children who have left the area but where there is no known information about a subsequent school to which the CTF can be sent. In these cases, the CTF should show XXXXXXX as the destination. If there are child protection concerns about the child, especially any previous history of them being on the register, the fact that they have disappeared must also be shared immediately with social services or the police, as the parent may be seeking to avoid detection following a serious incident of some kind.

The file will then be held in the LPD at the DfES, a secure Internet site, and, if the system is working properly, should that child then surface elsewhere, the information can be transferred to the relevant LA and school on request. If a child arrives at your school without their parent being able to give accurate details of their previous educational history and with no contact from a former school, a check on the LPD may provide the information. The new school can then contact a previous school to find out more. This is a relatively simple procedure but it does not yet appear to be standard practice.

Admissions procedures

The DfES guidance reiterates that of equal importance is the co-operation of schools over admissions, in accordance with local arrangements. Children who are missing out on education are not necessarily 'missing', they may be just unable to find a school place. This risks compounding difficulties that already exist and a commitment by all schools to ensuring that admission procedures are followed is essential. There is an unfortunate tendency to introduce arrangements for deciding whether or not to admit a pupil that may not be entirely legal and which can result in no provision being made available for months on end.

The assumption that the local authority will be able to make full-time alternative provision, without involving a school, is no longer appropriate. Every school must expect to operate through local partnerships and collaborations in future, perhaps even managing the out-of-school facility themselves until the admission has been sorted out. There is no central alternative available in many cases now that budgets are being devolved. It is a shared responsibility on us all, not just a problem for someone else.

A reluctance to participate in such co-ordinated admission arrangements where they have been agreed, even in 'hard to place' cases, must be a breach of any school's duty of care. Being the school that must offer a place, even if others can refuse, is an important role for community schools, not a burden. This is partly what such schools are for. Of course not every child is suitable for every school. If they are needed, learning or behaviour support and extra resources to facilitate a smooth transition are entirely reasonable requests that should be available as part of local protocols. Many local authorities now manage such issues through a representative panel, but this must not be allowed to introduce unreasonable delay or ignore the legal right of parents to express a preference.

Many children who cannot gain admission easily simply need a new start, even if they have already failed elsewhere. Some of them have been the unfortunate victims of a parental break-up, domestic violence or some other disruption in their lives that means they have had to change where they are living. Finding a new school is just a simple necessity which should be no more difficult for them to manage than their previous one. Hopefully things will improve for them once some stability returns. A long time out of school will only add to their problems. Some will have special needs that have been unmet by previous provision, but refusing to admit the child on such grounds alone is illegal. (Assessment should take place after admission, not before or as a condition of entry.) Unfortunately many pupils who are out of school are automatically assumed to present a problem when sometimes the difficulties are much more of our making than theirs.

Any assumption that all those in this position must all be accommodated in specialist units or alternative provision is clearly against the spirit of inclusion that is supposed to be a fundamental principle of the system. Many of them just need a school, but the longer it takes, the more complex their needs will become. Mainstream school staff should now have the skills and capacity to cope in all but a very few instances. Children who miss out because we have not made a place for them are being treated as badly as those children with SEN who used to be hidden away from sight. Such discrimination is just as unacceptable in its contemporary form.

The DfES guidance mentioned earlier provides a general framework within which individual decisions can then be made. If followed it would significantly reduce the risks of many children becoming disengaged from education. But these children need to be understood as individuals, or as members of particular groups who are known to be at risk. Because not all children are the same, some will require a different approach from what works for the majority. In many cases there is additional specialist guidance available, intended to promote their specific needs. The rest of this chapter introduces you to those who cannot be overlooked if we are serious about making a difference to what have been traditionally poor outcomes for far too long. What happens for these children will be one of the key tests of whether anything is really changing at all.

Looked-after children

Children in the care system, who are being 'looked after' by the local authority because their own parents cannot or will not do so, ought to be among those whose needs are being met most effectively. (There are about 60,000 nationally at any one time.) They should have armies of professionals looking out for them: social workers, foster carers, other care staff, advocates, mentors, teachers, even elected council members. They are at the top of everyone's priority list. But for many such children, coming into care, and staying there, seems only to compound the disasters that have already befallen them, especially in education. This has been something of national scandal but one which, at last, is now being addressed. Schools will need to be part of this new approach as never before (see also the DfES Green Paper *Care Matters*, 2006).

Under the Children Act 2004 s. 52, local authorities have a duty to promote the educational achievement of the children in their care. This includes:

- those who are on care orders through a court (Children Act 1989 s. 31 or s. 38);

- those who are accommodated voluntarily (s. 20);

- those subject to emergency orders for their immediate protection (s. 44 and s. 46);

- those who are accommodated compulsorily, remanded to the local authority or subject to criminal justice supervision orders with a residential requirement (s. 21).

This is a duty on the whole local authority, not just the education service. But, as the DfES guidance to governors, *Supporting Looked-After Learners* (January 2006) says about the duty on the elected council members who are, in effect these children's 'corporate parents':

> In order for them to implement this duty successfully, they will need the active co-operation of schools. School governing bodies have a major responsibility for helping children to succeed: they can champion their needs, raise awareness and challenge negative stereotypes (p. 4).

The last point is probably the most important. Children will be in the care system for a whole variety of reasons, but only about 2 per cent are detained because of something they have done wrong. Ironically, those who have committed serious offences who are in secure settings may well have greater educational opportunity than some of those still living in the community. Many will have complex special needs and other learning difficulties. Many are the victims of circumstances way beyond their control. Nonetheless, children in care often have a reputation that precedes them and which seems to lead to inevitable breaks in their education which we would certainly not tolerate for our own children. But they are 'our' children; or so we now have to think, especially if we too work for that same local authority or in one of the schools in its area.

There is a variety of reasons why looked-after children seem to end up out of education more than others:

- They may have been seriously mistreated previously with education given a low priority by their parents so that they cannot easily adjust to a normal school life on entering the care system.

- They are more likely to be excluded from school, and for longer periods. Further exclusion can also threaten their care placement and lead to more lengthy disruption.

- They may have long gaps in their educational history because of changes of address that have resulted in delays in new provision becoming available to them.

- They may not have had the sustained opportunity to study for GCSEs or may have missed the usual opportunities for routine testing, SATs, etc., so may not be placed in the right sets or study groups and become even more alienated as a result.

- They may have complex emotional needs, including mental health issues, problems with attachment, low self-esteem and a difficulty engaging in formal routines like school, homework, timetables, etc. which makes identifying suitable provision difficult.

- They may have been the victims of low educational expectations by those who now have responsibility for them because other issues in their lives have been seen as more pressing.

- There may be little practical support for study outside school, for example, as a result of a prevailing culture among other residents in a children's home that education is not for them.

School should be the place where some of the previous inadequacies and uncertainties in the child's life can be addressed. Looked-after children often say that they do not want to be seen as different. They want to blend in and be part of friendship groups like everyone else. This may well be why, in the past, school staff may not even have been aware of them. The balance between knowing about them but not singling them out as different is sometimes a difficult one. Much of the focus may need to be behind the scenes rather than any overt special emphasis that may make the child or young person feel uncomfortable. But this does not justify staff not being given full information by social workers about them, or schools not asking about their personal circumstances for fear of embarrassment or causing offence.

BEST PRACTICE FOR LOOKED-AFTER CHILDREN

Best practice for looked-after children would ensure that:

- key staff have an overview of the educational needs and progress of each looked-after child. (This may mean having to relate to more than one local authority, and being aware of the implications of their individual legal status);

- resources are allocated to match the needs and priorities according to clear policy commitments that are monitored in practice;

- it is clear who is responsible: the LAC co-ordinator or designated teacher should ideally be a member of the Senior Management Team;

- each looked-after child in the school has a Personal Education Plan (PEP) that has been arranged by the social worker and agreed with the school, child, foster carer, etc. This should set out targets and expectations for learning and be regularly reviewed and updated;

- the attendance of each child is closely monitored and every attempt made to deal quickly with any issues arising.

The LAC co-ordinator/designated teacher

The role of the school's LAC co–ordinator/designated teacher is especially important. It often happens that such a responsibility is simply added on to that of the SENCo (SEN co–ordinator). They may also be responsible for child protection as well. This is fine in theory. The jobs often overlap, as long as the role is properly recognised and resourced.

Similar skills are certainly required to do the job effectively. But it may be that this person's role as an advocate or champion for the child is difficult to reconcile with other functions, for example, those under the school's disciplinary system. Some schools have found it helpful to allocate a mentor or leaning support teacher to each looked-after child rather than trying to combine all the responsibilities in the same person. There may be a conflict of interest between what is best for the child and what may seem best for the school. Training to support such roles should be available.

It is especially important that someone has an eye to any risk of the child becoming disengaged from education. This would include, for example:

- ensuring a managed transition between Key Stages and other changes of school;
- responding quickly to any non-attendance;
- providing additional learning and homework support, etc.;
- pre-examination revision and help with managing coursework deadlines, etc.;
- trying to find alternatives to exclusion when the child has misbehaved;
- building strong links with the child's carers and social worker to promote their active participation in parents' evenings and school events, etc.

The aim is to ensure stability for the child wherever possible. These things do not happen by chance and a proactive approach that anticipates the possibility of problems is always to be preferred. The guidance about off-registration is especially important in this context. No such decision about a looked-after child should ever be made until all parties are agreed it is appropriate.

Targets

Local protocols may also mean that a looked-after child has additional priority for admission, over and above the normal arrangements. The Education Act 2005 s. 106 makes it a legal requirement that such systems are in place from September 2007. This may mean admitting a particular child even though the normal admission limit has been reached. There is a duty on the local authority to secure a place in a school, or other provision, within 20 days of the child becoming looked after. There is annual monitoring by the DfES of how many days' education every child has missed. No looked-after child should be losing more than 25 school days a year (for any reason). These challenging targets and rising expectations will inevitably increase the pressure on schools and admission authorities to make decisions quickly when required.

Most looked-after children are not missing from education, in the sense that we at least know where they are. Many are in residential placements with education provided, especially those with complex learning difficulties, but they may be a long way from home and easily forgotten. Their overall academic performance as a group is still disappointing. However, it is entirely unreasonable for the DfES to compare their performance with the general child population. The groups are nothing like each other; the looked-after population contains a far higher percentage of children who would not have been entered for any public examinations even if they were not in care. They would always have lagged behind in terms of academic performance. Some of the targets require looked-after children as a group to do better in examinations than their peers as a whole in that local authority! That is a nonsense when as many as 50 per cent may have learning disabilities or profound and complex needs.

But what does matter is that being in care should not compound the child's problems. We must recognise that this particular group of children will contain many of those with the most social problems that are bound to make educational participation difficult for them. Meeting their needs now that they are being looked after is essentially about preventing them from becoming missing in the future, with all the consequences that result when that happens. The chance for us to resolve things may end in many cases once they are 16+. The longer-term impact of how much we have managed to achieve so far will, for them, be only just beginning.

Privately fostered children

Although it took some time for the implications to become clear, Victoria Climbié was a privately fostered child, i.e. she was allegedly being cared for by someone other than her parents, but without the intervention of social services in making the placement. Any such arrangement should be reported to the local authority for a child under 16, or under 18 if he/she is disabled. For various reasons, many children are in this position and there is a growing awareness that their welfare may not always be adequately protected. Improving the quality of support for them and their carers is part of the specific responsibilities of the new Local Safeguarding Children Boards (LSCB).

Of course many such children are perfectly safe, but there has traditionally been little awareness of them by outside agencies. There is a risk that some at least may not be engaging in education because we do not know that they are there. Privately fostered children are a diverse group but those about whom we might be most concerned include:

- those who have come from overseas, legally or illegally, but without their parents;
- children whose parents have made private care arrangements with someone else who is not an immediate relative;
- teenagers who have broken ties with their parents and moved in with another family;
- young people of school age living semi-independently under the loose supervision of an adult to whom they are not related.

Working Together to Safeguard Children (2006)

This document states that:

> Teachers, health and other professionals should notify the local authority of a private fostering arrangement that comes to their attention, where they are not satisfied that the local authority have been or will be notified of the arrangement. (para. 11.13)

Under Part IX and Schedule 8 of the Children Act 1989, with certain exemptions where close family members are involved, both the parent and the prospective carer are required to notify the local authority of their intention so that an assessment of the child's circumstances can be made, ideally, before the placement starts. This has traditionally been a rather low priority, but new requirements under section 44 of the Children Act 2004 should now mean that the inspection arrangements are made more widely known and that advice and support are offered as required. Arrangements being made for the child's education should be part of any such assessment.

Do not assume that someone else must have told the local authority about the child. Relevant school staff should be aware of whom to contact. Nothing happens unless someone takes responsibility for making sure that it does. Notification may be done by use of the Common Assessment Framework but where there are grounds for thinking that the health or development of the child may be at risk of significant harm, consideration should be given to a more urgent referral under child protection procedures (see Chapter 4).

Of particular concern may be the arrangements for children coming from overseas to be educated in the UK and who are living with people who are not members of their immediate family. School staff should check carefully, before admitting the child, whether they are here on an educational visa. This may sound a perfectly reasonable basis for them to be admitted, but such visas often specify that the child may not be admitted to a state school but is coming to this country in order to be educated in the private sector only (i.e. not at public expense).

There have been several examples where parents appeared to be paying carers for the provision of a private education that was in fact being provided free, or where the young people, even those under 16, were effectively living in bedsits with a landlord rather than with a proper carer. Any such concern should be reported under child protection procedures. Action must also be taken if there is any suggestion that a child or young person of compulsory school age is not accessing education, for example, because they are engaged in domestic service, illegal employment, etc.

Other vulnerable groups

Gypsies and travellers

Guidance from the DfES can be found in *Aiming High: Raising the Achievement of Gypsy/Traveller Pupils – A Guide to Good Practice* (0443/2003). There is a significant amount of work being undertaken by local authorities and schools to promote the education of children from the gypsy and traveller community. In most areas Traveller Education Services are available to support those children who are currently out of school. They will also work with those schools with significant numbers of travellers where additional learning support or special arrangements for home–school liaison may needed. It is important to remember in this context that 'education' does not necessarily require a school and that some parents may choose to educate their children in other ways. But the inclusion agenda seeks to promote as much participation as possible and to build bridges between communities where tensions may exist in a local area.

Many of the traditional traveller occupations have disappeared in recent years and there has been a general reluctance by local authorities to provide sufficient sites for them to live on. This lack of recognition does not mean the communities, and their children, no longer exist, but it may mean they have to keep moving. The Criminal Justice and Public Order Act 1994 effectively removed the previous duty to make provision for travellers, and the consequent shortage of more permanent sites has undoubtedly made it more difficult both for parents and local authorities to fulfil their respective educational duties.

Schools and examination curricula require stability in their pupils' wider lives over years at a time. Children need continuity in their living arrangements if they are to attend regularly. For these children, sustained participation through courses that last for two or more years can therefore be almost impossible. Young people and their parents lose motivation and their resulting performance in public examinations is inevitably disappointing.

Coupled with what would be seen as racist attitudes if they were exhibited towards other groups, and some traveller parents at least who are deliberately seeking to evade their responsibilities, there are plenty of reasons to be gloomy about the hope of bringing about much improvement. Local authority children's services plans should promote the rights of all children to receive education and aim to combat inequalities of all kinds, without distinction. Sometimes only alternative provision is realistic, perhaps even delivered on the site where they are living, especially with older children and young people. But where schools have the opportunity to provide services, they need to be ready and willing to do so. Every school needs to develop an awareness of any local issues and encourage respect for minority lifestyles, whether or not they have traveller or gypsy children themselves at present. Every pupil will form part of the opinion-forming adult community of the future.

SCHOOL SELF-REVIEW

The school improvement process and various forms of self-review provide ample opportunity to promote the effective learning of minority groups, including travellers. For example:

- Are staff aware of any traveller children?

- Is their culture celebrated and valued?

- Do admissions policies recognise their individual needs and is differentiated learning available which may have to fit round the fact that the child only attends for part of the year?

- Is transport made available where it is legally required and are the services available through the local Traveller Education Service used as necessary, especially where pupils have learning difficulties or require additional support?

- Can the school provide any services to parents that will help them to overcome what will probably have been unhappy experiences when they were young? (See also Chapter 6.)

Travellers are all individuals and should never be approached as if they were all identical, on the basis of either personal prejudice or bad experiences encountered previously with other traveller children. Legal powers to enforce attendance may still have to be used if required. There is no special dispensation open to them, other than the allowance that can be made to authorise absence because the child is currently away from the area. But are the procedures being used fairly, recognising, for example, parents' possible problems with literacy or the unreliability of receiving post when you have no formal address? Such work is far from easy, and not always successful, but it should always be attempted.

Asylum-seekers, refugees and homeless children

Guidance from the DfES can be found in *Aiming High: Guidance on Supporting the Education of Asylum-Seeking and Refugee Children* (0287/2004). While most asylum-seeking children arrive with one or both of their parents, some do not. They may arrive with other adults or relatives who fail to protect their interests, or they may even be unaccompanied. Asylum-seekers who have made the necessary application to remain can get help with accommodation and essential living needs from the National Asylum Support Service (NASS). Children in these families then have the right to access healthcare and full rights to participate in education. They are also entitled to free school meals, school milk and special uniform grants because their parents or carers are not permitted to work and support themselves while their application is being considered.

Local authorities are required by section 14 of the Education Act 1996 to provide education for all children in their area. The guidance says that they should seek to ensure that there are no unreasonable delays in securing the admission of asylum-seeking and refugee pupils to schools. Admission procedures should be the same as for any other pupils, even allowing for the fact that many are likely to have little spoken English, at least to begin with. There should be local policies and procedures in place to address their needs. Most authorities will have a dedicated support service available either as part of a wider service for vulnerable minority groups or specifically aimed at these families in particular. This may include help with translation, interpreting and practical information about procedures for admitting a child to a school.

The security of regular school attendance can be an important therapeutic response for children who have experienced a significant trauma prior to arrival in the UK, especially for younger children. Asylum-seeking families have the same entitlement to Early Years provision as UK residents and this can be especially important in helping them to learn English and making links with health visitors, doctors, etc. Being in an education setting opens many doors that are otherwise likely to be difficult to access. For older young people, nearing the end of compulsory schooling, alternatives to school may be more appropriate, but this should not be assumed. It may sometimes be more suitable for them to attend a National Curriculum Year below their chronological Year, provided they are still within the range of compulsory school age.

BEST PRACTICE GUIDANCE

The DfES guidance offers a range of practical advice and strategies to assist schools in managing provision for such children, from ideas for sensory and practical play to use of drama and toys. Where children are living in hostel accommodation, sometimes with stressed or otherwise emotionally damaged parents who cannot be expected to have the confidence to play with their children themselves or support their learning, the benefits of being in school are incalculable. Rapid enrolment and support for regular attendance are especially important in this context. See also www.nrif.org.uk, the website of the National Refugee Integration Forum, which was established by the Home Office in 2000 to bring together representatives from the voluntary and statutory sectors to explore practical ways to improve integration and share good practice. This is well worth a look if this area of work is not a regular activity for your school or if there are few support services in the locality.

For some other children and young people, issues around access to education may arise because they have had to leave their home with a parent after domestic violence or because of eviction. Teenagers may have become estranged from their parents while still under school-leaving age. These are a crucial group for co-ordinated responses from agencies in order to ensure that continuity of education can be maintained if at all possible. Changing address need not necessarily mean changing school, though that often seems to be assumed. Flexibility may be required about time-keeping, uniform, homework and other normal school routines. Assistance may be needed with transport or help in claiming benefits.

Where children are living in hostels or other forms of temporary accommodation, there will often be a support worker or volunteer seeking to maintain contact with their school and to encourage the child's continued participation. Where changes of school are unavoidable, wherever possible they need to be properly managed in the child's best interests, not be a reactive consequence of decisions that have already been made without consultation. It sounds obvious but it often does not happen and the child can then be out of education just at the time when they need it most.

Pregnant girls of school age and other health issues

Similar issues can arise for pregnant schoolgirls or others who have medical needs that may lead to gaps in their education. Teenage pregnancy is still higher in the UK than in many of its European partners. It should not necessarily mean that the girl can no longer be in school, any more than it means a teacher having to stop work immediately. School nurses or other health advisors will be key partners who will be able to offer practical support and advice, with the young person's consent. Pregnancy does, however, have to be managed, both as a health and safety responsibility for the mother, unborn child and other pupils, and as an inclusion issue, if indeed the school is made aware of it, which does not always happen.

It is, unfortunately, often the case that early pregnancy runs in families and may be a major factor in repeating the social exclusion experienced over several generations. Everything a school does by way of relationship and sex education, information about contraception advice and general health promotion, will make a significant contribution in itself to promoting wider social inclusion. It can suggest alternatives to lifestyles that may appear to the child to be almost inevitable. This is another area where prevention is so much better than responding only in a crisis.

A decision to keep the baby will have enormous implications for the mother's future participation in employment or education. Trying to make sure that she does not fall behind, almost as a matter of course, is essential. Some local authorities offer specific support services for schoolgirl mothers-to-be and for those who want to remain in education once the baby is born. (Some also provide support for young fathers.) Not many schools can offer child care or crèche facilities that may be more readily available in the further education sector, but school attendance can often still be managed through part-time or distance learning arrangements. Access to public examinations is especially important for those who become pregnant during Years 10 and 11. Having a baby and achieving GCSEs are not mutually exclusive alternatives.

There is a range of other medical issues that will need careful management in order to help pupils with health problems to participate in school as much as possible. There are sometimes obstacles presented to effective inter-agency working by unnecessarily cautious concerns about confidentiality. Parents may be told by doctors or others that the child should not attend school when this is not, in fact, necessary. This whole issue can become an excuse for not thinking laterally, even accepting that health colleagues often have a rather higher standard of privacy to meet than others. But there should be no reason for not sharing information if this is intended to promote the child's participation in education. If consent from parents or the child is required, then it should be obtained as a matter of routine, not be seen as an insurmountable obstacle. Too high an emphasis on confidentiality can effectively deny children access to appropriate provision.

Children with additional health needs can become children missing education when other ways of working, keeping their needs at the centre, could have avoided it. Temporary adaptations to the curriculum and timetable can be made. Special arrangements for transport can be authorised by the local authority where the pupil has had an accident or has restricted mobility. Some teachers have been unwilling to administer medication or manage a child's medical needs, because they feel that the risks involved, to themselves or to the pupil, are too great. This caution is understandable but it should not lead to the child being, in effect, informally excluded. Specialist support and advice should always be available and school staff should never be made to feel that they have been left to deal with such complex concerns on their own. But most situations are entirely manageable within schools' health management policies.

Clear agreements with parents, and with the young person concerned, about who is responsible for what, are of course essential. A written Individual Health Care Plan may be required. If the priority is seen as maintaining the child's access to education, solutions can usually be found with goodwill on all sides. Blanket policies based on unnecessary professional sensitivities, the fear of subsequent litigation or basing decisions on irrational or preconceived fears about the condition involved, are not an appropriate basis for decision-making. Risks can be managed even if they cannot be entirely removed, as with many potentially risky situations in school life such as a school trip abroad or taking part in hazardous sports.

Young offenders

Dealing with young offenders is a high government priority in response to those who present a risk to their local communities, to others and to themselves. There is growing concern about the extent of offending behaviour, including the sexual abuse by children of other children and other serious or violent offences. The widespread abuse of illegal drugs and alcohol is certainly a factor and children are coming to the attention of agencies at ever younger ages. But that may be a good thing as services can then be made available before it is too late. Key school staff need to be aware of the specialist agencies in their locality, including the Youth Offending Team or Service, and services provided through the voluntary and health sectors. This will enable them to assist in multi-agency responses that may prevent more serious problems occurring later.

Damaged and damaging young people still need to receive an education. Even if their needs may have been well met while in custody or a secure residential unit, most come back to their families, communities, and therefore to their local schools eventually. Those sentenced to less than 4 months' detention must, for example, remain on the roll of their school ready for their return. They can be marked as 'present' (approved educational activity off-site) in the meantime. But many more are dealt with in ways that mean that they continue to remain at home as before. Young people are never sentenced to be denied an education but this often seems to be an unfortunate consequence that only compounds their disaffection and risks reinforcing their offending.

School staff will want to be active partners in preventive programmes such as Youth Inclusion and Support Panels (YISPs) in order to address the challenges posed by their pupils. Some offenders may not be appropriate for full-time attendance in mainstream schools. Some will need a co-ordinated and integrated programme that is designed to address both their offending behaviour and their typical under-performance in education. Increasingly, schools may also be involved in programmes to address the deficit in their parenting, through Parenting Contracts and Orders either agreed voluntarily or imposed by courts. Where there is interplay with breaches of the school's disciplinary standards it is especially important that conditions imposed by courts about, for example, regular school attendance, are not unwittingly undermined by denying them the opportunity to attend.

The Youth Offending Teams have key targets relating to education as part of the overall strategy to reduce offending and manage risk. Measure 10, for example of the relevant standards, requires a YOT to ensure that 90 per cent of the young offenders it is working with are engaged in either full-time education, training or employment. For those still of school age this clearly cannot be done by the YOT alone. Although these are specific youth justice targets, there is a sense in which all services are subject to this expectation if it is to be achieved. The fact that many offenders have no access to regular educational provision is often highlighted by inspections but there are clearly tensions to be resolved if the young person's lifestyle is not compatible with the routines that schools quite reasonably require. Proper planning for their needs is obviously essential, but often does not seem to happen very effectively.

PUBLIC PROTECTION ARRANGEMENTS

A small group of offenders who pose a risk to children will require more intensive local monitoring under the Multi-Agency Public Protection Arrangements (MAPPA). This process normally relates to adults, including new procedures for informing headteachers of the existence of 'Approved Premises' (hostels) accommodating convicted offenders or those on bail, where they are in the immediate vicinity of a school or nursery. Despite regular furore in the press, this does not include disclosing the names and details of individuals and is unlikely to do so in the future. An approach such as 'Megan's Law' in the USA that makes information more widely available tends to drive offenders underground, with the result that registration rates, and therefore the level of supervision, is much lower than in the UK. This just increases the risk to children.

There will also be special procedures in place where those under 18 have already been convicted or cautioned for such offences. They can be registered as sex or violent offenders from the age of 10. Education is not routinely represented in the arrangements for adults, unless a specific risk to children at school is identified. But for juveniles there is clearly a need to manage such arrangements in a way that also addresses their educational needs. The Youth MAPPA panel, at which education officers will always be present, provides a regular opportunity for any local issues to be addressed and for informed discussion about the individuals concerned.

Headteachers can expect to be made aware of any current pupil, or potential pupil, who is subject to such supervision. Full consultation should take place about the level of identified risk if it proposed that they are to remain in mainstream education. This is not necessarily as worrying as it sounds. The risk, for example, may have been substantially reduced by subsequent therapeutic work since the offence or may never have been an issue for other children of similar age. There should be no attempt at subterfuge or partial deceit about a young person's circumstances. But in return colleagues in other agencies will expect school staff to handle such information responsibly. Decisions must be based on that particular individual and any actual risk he/she may pose, rather than based on any pre-conceived assumptions or the outcomes for other children in the past.

Home-educated pupils

As indicated in Chapter 2, not all children and young people have to go to school, because their parents have chosen to educate them 'otherwise'. This is a perfectly legal alternative that has always been the case since education became compulsory in the nineteenth century. Not all parents wish to use the school system, either the state or the private sector, in order to ensure that their child is educated. It could even be argued that with the advent of the Internet, teaching your child yourself is now easier than ever and children who are disaffected with school might benefit from the arrangement. Some religious groups and individuals still take this option as well as it being appropriate for some children with health difficulties or those parents who wish to ensure that their child is taught according to a particular ethos. This causes no problems for the children in many cases but may lead to them becoming rather isolated from their wider peers.

The local authority has a role in monitoring such arrangements, though the legal basis to their involvement is unclear. They have to ensure that all children are 'properly educated', including in accordance with any SEN issues. Home-educating parents still have a right to an assessment and even a statement if it is needed. So it has to be a teacher who decides whether the education is adequate. Local authorities should have a named officer with this responsibility as at least part of their work. But they may have very little information on which to base their judgement and ultimately a court may even have to be asked to decide.

As there is no required curriculum, the only test of whether the provision made by parents is legal is whether or not it is 'suitable' to the child's needs. There is no defined number of hours that must be involved or specified content. It has been held in the past that the legal test is met if the education provided seeks to prepare the child for the adult life of the community of which he/she is a member. Bearing in mind that not many adults make daily use of algebraic formulas or knowledge of life under the Tudors and Stuarts, the content of such an education may look very different from what is available at a school. On what basis then can it be judged 'unsuitable'? Such arguments with parents can drag on for ever.

A School Attendance Order would be required to force parents to re-register the child once they are no longer on any school's Admission Register, or if they have never been on one. These are usually applied for through the Education Welfare Service (see

Chapter 2). However, many of these parents will be elusive and less than co-operative. Considerable persistence may be required. This is another reason why the removal of pupils from the Admission Register of a school without proper procedures may make things very difficult. Parents who are home-educating are, of course, free to change their minds and may choose to re-admit the child to the school system at any time, perhaps in order to take GCSEs etc. They are still entitled to a school place just like anyone else.

An Order, once issued by the local authority, names the school to which the parent must admit the pupil immediately. So there must therefore be a school willing to admit them. The child will almost certainly need considerable support in engaging with the curriculum, possibly for the first time. Where children have never previously been part of the school system, or where they have never been taught the basics that participation normally requires, this will clearly be a process that will require great sensitivity and a focus on supporting the child individually. This is effectively an SEN issue even if the child has no learning disability as traditionally understood. Such reintegration will need to be carefully planned across a range of professionals to ensure an effective and co-ordinated response.

Of particular concern will be those children whose parents may claim to be educating them at home but who are clearly not doing so. This will be especially concerning with children who have never been to school, if the child may have un-assessed learning needs, if the parent has mental health problems or if they provide a generally poor standard of care. These situations risk the child suffering 'significant harm' to both their immediate and longer-term health and development.

In situations like these wider questions of both child protection and potential supervision or care proceedings may have to be considered. The local authority may even consider seeking an Education Supervision Order under the Children Act 1989. These are rare but they do give officers the power to give directions to the parent, which can be an offence if not followed. This action may be sufficient to persuade them to agree to a change of provision.

Conclusion

Social and educational inclusion is really put to the test in circumstances such as all these. If education were a gift rather than an entitlement for all, perhaps we might not need to have anything like this range of potential gaps as part of our thinking. It is easy, when you are based in a school, to think only of the needs of those who are there. Local authority officers have not always been very popular with their teacher colleagues when asked to consider their wider responsibilities towards other children. This reluctance is entirely understandable.

But those who are not there may not be anywhere else either. What we are all doing about them will be a key 'Every Child Matters' indicator. It may be necessary for school staff to change their perspective or at least to recognise that those championing the cause of these children are not trying to be difficult. They are just trying to make sure that we actually do what we have promised to do for those children who need us most. We are all supposed to be on the same side – theirs!

Making a positive contribution

At last, somebody's starting to listen. I've always wanted to have my say but I didn't know how to do it. The trouble with social workers and teachers and all the rest is that they spend all their time talking about me, to me or at me. They have endless meetings when I'm not there but never give me a chance to say what I want to say. They're nice enough most of the time, but nothing ever changes – except the social workers of course. Mine changes every other week! I really liked the last one. That's the trouble with being young – they think you don't have any brains at all! Not that they seemed to listen to my mum that much either. But, fair's fair, they have got better recently. Let's hope it lasts.

Missing out

This book has been about those children, and their parents, who are the most difficult group to engage in education; the 'rhinos' as a school I used to work with called them (Really Here In Name Only), and the others who have proved resistant to all our initial hopes and expectations. It is immensely frustrating when families do not respond to what we have to offer: when we make appointments to see them they're not there. Or, when we have tried to be as flexible as we can about timekeeping, uniform, curriculum and so on, they still don't seem to be able to deliver on all the promises that were made. It can feel like endlessly going round over the same old arguments with no real progress to show for all our efforts. I was once presented by a school with a blank photograph frame. The names of three children that I had completely failed to get to attend were printed at the bottom, marked 'Ben's Class of '91'! I do know how difficult it can be.

In situations like these, it is easy to become disillusioned and to feel there is little point in bothering. But it is essential not lose sight of both the moral and the educational imperative to meet these children's needs. I don't think I could still do some of the endlessly patient work that some colleagues, who are more in the front line than I am, have to do every day. It is something of a luxury to be able to stand back from the daily duties, but we all need to do it now and again. This book is not about telling already skilled people how to do their job. What I hope I can do is to offer an opportunity for reflection that may open a few windows and let in a bit of fresh air. It is so easy to become stale.

Legal solutions sometimes have to be relied upon because nothing else is possible, like prosecution of parents for unauthorised absences and formal exclusions. But we know that these interventions rarely, if ever, make much difference on their own. If it were that simple everyone would do it all the time and every problem would be resolved.

People under pressure rarely respond positively when placed under even more pressure – ask any busy teacher. These children and parents might tell you the same, if anybody asked them.

Somehow we have to find new ways of working, not just shout the old ways in ever-louder voices. The kinds of patronising and unequal relationships that professional people used to have with members of 'the public' and with their children are no longer acceptable. Perhaps they used to do as they were told without question, but they are wiser now, our 'customers', who have to be understood as individuals. The same has been true for doctors, clergy, politicians, police officers and a whole host of other people in authority, not just teachers. The old ways, if they ever really existed, can no longer be sustained.

Some of us may regret the loss of a time when the teacher was always right: respected both by the pupils and by their parents, who rarely darkened the doors beyond the carol concert and the annual prize-giving and just left us to it. I suppose our perspective depends in part on what kind of school we worked in during those so-called halcyon days. Or, more likely, what kind of school we went to ourselves, which was probably not entirely typical of the community as whole. It is always essential to distinguish between our professional and personal selves in order to be sure that we are not being affected by factors in our own lives that we may have scarcely recognised, let alone taken account of.

In the real world, not everyone is pleased with what goes on at their children's school all the time. Headteachers are still seen as effective leaders and role-models by most people. But those who don't normally get asked for their views may sometimes wonder why schools seem to shut so often when they still have to go to work or find childcare. Why does going in to see someone about their child still feel like it did when they were 14! And then they have the cheek to criticise you for going away as a family in the only week you can afford it or the factory shuts down, just because it happens to be in term-time. School is not necessarily a happy place to go, even as a parent, especially if you think you are likely to be told off. Life is complicated and what is happening at school is only one area that adults have to deal with, not the sole focus of the day for everyone.

Parents and children have views and opinions and want to have them heard, even if those views reflect a minority or even a deviant viewpoint as far as we are concerned. People are no longer prepared to be deferential in the presence of a professional and to accept the word of experts without question. The nature of the parental relationship, and the growing sense that children and young people too have an entirely legitimate perspective on their own lives, demands new kinds of working relationships that are more reflective of the expectations of society as a whole. Schools cannot be oases of ordered authority when all else around is in chaos, no matter how much we might wish that they were.

The Ofsted guidance that started all this, *Evaluating Education Inclusion* (2000), recognised that the quality of a school's relationship with its parents and pupils was the heart of the issue. Inclusion is not only about what curriculum we offer or what policies we have in place. It's also about what it feels like when you walk through the door or whether it is clear from your first meeting with staff that it's parents like you and children like yours that the staff are genuinely interested in. If not, then we are losing before we start. The guidance specifically asked inspectors to pay attention to the parents on the margins and ask them what they think of the school. They should even search out the views of the children who were not there during the inspection. Fine words, but I doubt this happens, especially now that some last no longer than a day.

But every child in the school (and in the wider community) deserves to have their needs met. At this point, we are concerned only about those who might miss out – there are plenty of other opportunities to work with all the rest. What can we do to try and move beyond all the negativity and blame, on both sides, and into a relationship to which our customers can make a more positive contribution? It's a tough call and of course it won't always work out. But maybe we haven't spent as much time as we should in thinking about whether the obstacles to better relationships that lie with us have been addressed. We need to make sure that every possible opportunity has been taken to be more creative in our approach. Surely it must be worth the effort?

Children

Helping children and young people to make a positive contribution to society, both now and in the future, is at the heart of *Every Child Matters*. This is no longer about doing things 'to' or 'for' children, but with them, as partners. Of course we have already come a considerable distance in terms of collective opportunities for participation. School councils are now part of life, even in some infant schools. Millennium Volunteers have made a significant contribution to the management of projects for the environment, even spending budgets that have been overseen by youth workers. Children have been trained as peer mentors, learning supporters, advocates and friends of children with special needs and disabilities. They get their own Ofsted report and are beginning to make a contribution to the appointment of the adult staff that will be working with them, expressing opinions and exercising choice. All of these activities are immensely important contributions that they themselves can make towards the achievement of the five outcomes, ready for their adult life.

MAKING A POSITIVE CONTRIBUTION

Children and their parents must be enabled to:

- engage in decision-making and support the community and environment
- engage in law-abiding and positive behaviour in and out of school
- develop positive relationships and choose not to bully and discriminate
- develop self-confidence and successfully deal with significant life changes and challenges
- develop enterprising behaviour

DfES, *Every Child Matters: Change for Children in Schools* (2004)

This commitment to participation is not about always giving children what they want. It is not about allowing children and young people to make all the decisions so that we don't have to, or ignoring the fact that their age and understanding may still mean that they do not always appreciate their own best interests. Some of the things children do, like bullying, not telling the truth or thinking only of themselves, have to be challenged in a school community, even if they are allowed elsewhere. Children must still be children, not smaller adults. But they are entitled to be treated with respect as individuals; listened to and not just tolerated; both seen and heard so that they can practise the skills that will be so valuable to them when they are older.

Listening to children has not always had as high a priority in school as it has had for other professionals for whom the Children Act 1989 has always been the most significant piece of legislation. This Act has often been misinterpreted, whether by accident or design. It did not say that the 'wishes' of children were paramount, but their 'welfare'. The two are not always compatible. But it was supposed to change the focus of parents, courts and social workers. Children are not adults' property or 'objects of concern' to be argued over or decided about. They are individuals with a perspective to share and a contribution to make. How could they do that if no one ever thought to tell them what was happening, ask them what they thought or give them an opportunity to be consulted? The fact that the views of the pupil concerned, for example, might never be heard at an exclusion appeal attended only by their parents, governors and the school staff, now seems an unsustainable anachronism.

We have had to get used to the fact that children and young people will be at the review about them, maybe even attend the safeguarding meeting or have someone there specifically to speak for them. Their views will count when we are consulting on some new procedure that affects their lives. It may have caused some waves when Ofsted started to share the findings of inspections with the children whose school it is, but that is entirely consistent with thinking elsewhere. The new Joint Area Reviews (JAR) of local authorities have a similar emphasis. Children and young people can't make a positive contribution of this kind, or be encouraged to make positive contributions to society as a whole, if they don't have the opportunity to do so as a routine part of school life.

This is a significant challenge, especially when thinking about those who are socially excluded. Schools have traditionally been built on clear hierarchies and structures of authority in which everybody knew their place. The Children Act 1989 questioned such assumptions and asked professionals to take their clients and 'service users' much more seriously. This was intended to avoid catastrophes like Cleveland. The abuse of the children's rights was seen as coming as much from the inflexible and insensitive actions of those who were supposed to protect them as from their parents. The professionals took little time to consult the children concerned, or indeed their parents, about the implications of the decisions they were making or how the concerns could best be dealt with from the children's perspective and at least cost to them.

'Dude, where's my outcomes?'

This intriguing question is the title of a chapter by an Anglo-American team, Mark Friedman, Louise Garnett and Mike Pinnock, in *Safeguarding and Promoting the Well-being of Children, Families and Communities* (Jane Scott and Harriet Ward (eds), Jessica Kingsley, 2005). It asks us to consider the importance of the voice of the child, among other factors, when assessing the effectiveness of our work. The Children Act 2004 is all about outcomes. It's not what we do that matters, it's what we achieve. The chapter considers the importance of partnership, between professionals and, crucially with clients, as the most meaningful way of ensuring accountability.

Education professionals should be entirely comfortable with this. We measure what we do all the time by the performance of the children and by the views of their parents about the quality of what we provide. But those families and individuals who are focus of this book are often not included in our analysis. Their voices may not be heard. They are in the 'other' category or are seen only as part of the percentage which, while hopefully getting smaller, still never features in our key performance indicators because they have little or nothing to show for their last eleven years.

They are seen as the inevitable failures of the system, both our failure and their own, because their measurable outcomes are so poor. The young people I am concerned about here may not be entered for the exams or are not even still in the school system by then. What hope then is there of reversing the spiral of social inclusion for them as individuals? They will have views about their own lives that we have probably not even considered in the face of the pressures on schools to perform in measurable terms. But what has happened for them has to become a test of our performance as well, just as significant as the achievements of those at the other end of the spectrum. If we haven't delivered for them, we haven't really delivered.

The chapter by Friedman *et al.* suggests that the perception of the service users, in this context, the children, is all-important. There needs to be constant dialogue, even with those who will not talk to us! We have to create opportunities for participation, even by those who will not attend the meeting! Perhaps we will need entirely new ways of trying to understand what the barriers are, before those who are disengaged are too easily dismissed as not interested. Children do have views, if not always the ones we want to hear. They may not always use the mechanisms for expressing them that we say they should. But they have an understanding of what works for them and what doesn't. That may actually be more important than what we think if we are to make any difference.

CHILDREN'S COMMISSIONERS

New ways of hearing what children have to say are emerging through the national and local Children's Commissioners. While these bodies aim to provide a voice for all children and young people on a wide range of issues that affect their lives, they have a special focus on those who might otherwise not have the skills or opportunity to speak through existing mechanisms:

England	http://www.childrenscommissioner.org/
Wales	http://www.childcom.org.uk/
Scotland	http://www.sccyp.org.uk/
N. Ireland	http://www.niccy.org.uk/

The liveliest websites seem to be the Welsh one (available in both languages) and 'Niccy', based around a cartoon dog. Both of these have a range of interactive activities, resources and services to help keep children safe and give them a voice in their local communities. There has been some disappointment at the slow progress in England, but Professor (now Sir) Al Aynsley-Green and other staff are in post and the website has recently been revamped. The extent to which these officials will offer vulnerable and marginalised children access to the services they need is still an open question, but, bearing in mind they were set up as a response to the Victoria Climbié case, this must surely be a priority.

Some local authorities have now begun to appoint their own Commissioners or other children's rights workers who will certainly have a particular interest in schools as the largest arena in which children need the opportunity to participate. They often relate primarily to enabling contributions to service-planning by looked-after children but may also be involved in other local campaigns or consultations. These roles may include running focus groups, conducting surveys, facilitating young people's contributions to meetings, conferences and reports and generally responding to the concerns raised by the children and young people in their area.

The Children's Workforce

Every professional needs to be adopting this approach all the time, not assuming that it will be done only by those with a specific brief to represent children's interests. Marginalising the issue to a footnote on the agenda is not sufficient. 'Effective communication and engagement' is, for example, the first element of the new Common Core of Skills and Knowledge for the Children's Workforce. It is worth quoting at some length as few people will actually have read it:

> Good communication is central to working with children, young people, their families and carers. It is a fundamental part of the Common Core. It involves, listening, questioning, under-standing and responding to what is being communicated by children, young people and those caring for them. It is important to be able to communicate both on a one-to-one basis and in a group context. Communication is not just about the words you use, but also your manner of speaking, body language and, above all, the effectiveness with which you listen. To communicate effectively it is important to take account of culture and context, for example, where English is an additional language.
>
> Effective engagement requires the involvement of children, young people and those caring for them in the design and delivery of services and decisions that affect them. It is important to consult with them and consider their opinions and perspectives from the outset. A key part of effective communication and engagement is trust, both between the workforce, children, young people and their carers, and between and within different sectors of the workforce itself. To build a rapport . . . it is important to demonstrate understanding, respect and honesty. Continuity in relationships promotes engagement and the improvement of lives.

(DfES, *Common Core of Skills and Knowledge for the Children's Workforce*, 2005)

These general principles are then developed further under key headings:

- listening and building empathy
- summarising and explaining
- consultation and negotiation
- knowing how communication works
- understanding confidentiality and ethics
- knowing the sources of support
- knowing the importance of respect.

These skills will already be largely familiar to any teacher of course, but the sense of being part of a common workforce that shares these approaches may not yet have been fully understood. It is still early days for the new generic Children Services authorities that now include both education and social care workers. But all schools must ensure that they are an integral part of local services, not separate from them, so that this ethos is consistent across all service providers in a local area.

Very similar commitments can be found in the National Service Framework for those working in health services, including leaflets for children and young people to reinforce the point. Teachers have had their own workforce reform in recent years, but that has been much more about their own terms and conditions of employment and should not be confused with this attempt to define the kinds of professional relationships that all those who work with children should share.

Complaints

New arrangements have come into force from September 2006 through which children and young people in receipt of services can make complaints and representations about those who provide them. These provisions, which are statutory, relate only to social care services provided under the Children Act 1989 – care, supervision, adoption, children in need assessments, etc. Local authorities must have a Complaints Manager to oversee progress according to defined timescales. It is disappointing that, at this stage, complaints about schools or the way in which educational professionals have carried out their functions are not included in this particular procedure.

However, schools must have their own complaints procedures that should be available to both parents and children. In time, with the growing sense of one workforce embracing what were previously separate departments, it seems highly likely that a similar system will need to be in place across all local services, including education. This has already happened with respect to allegations against any children's professional who may have abused a child or put them at risk of 'significant harm'. Teachers are subject to exactly the same procedure as social workers, foster carers and others. Learning about both your rights and responsibilities as an individual, and how to complain effectively, are certainly key elements of responsible citizenship. They also empower children and young people to keep themselves safe more effectively.

Thinking creatively

We will all need some imagination to engage with the children who may not easily respond to other opportunities. Here are a few modest suggestions that teachers and school managers might like to consider in order to make sure that the paper commitment to consult with all children and help them make a contribution can be demonstrated in routine practice:

- Talk to children where they are (physically, emotionally, linguistically) rather than expecting them to come to us all the time. Dialogue does not all have to take place when they are in school as this immediately sets a structure which some will find inhibiting.

- Let the pupil choose where the meeting about them takes place and who is there, rather than having all those decisions made for them by others in advance.

- Establish a charter mark or standard for school policies and procedures that can demonstrate there has been effective engagement and consultation with the pupils. Print them with a 'pupil approved' logo that shows they have reached this standard which others without the mark have not.

- Use IT endlessly, the only means of communication that most young people use. Send text messages to confirm appointments (with suitable safeguards agreed with parents) or, at a more general level, to test out pupils' opinions where choices are involved. Get the pupils to create webpages and Internet 'blogs' to generate conversations or set up something like 'BackChat' on the Welsh Commissioner's site that encourages children and young people to share their views and ideas.

- Allow the pupils to dictate the agenda for a staff INSET session for once, with staff listening to what they want to say about the school and discussing what they want to discuss.

- Include pupils on working groups when considering new policies that affect them and ask them how we might best involve the rest of the school community in taking any change forward.

- Tear up all the rules now and again about how things are usually done with a challenging or difficult pupil and give them the chance to say what could be done differently to help them participate. Look upon it as no different from having to make physical adaptations for the child with restricted mobility. What other kinds of adaptations does this child need us to make in order to get them in?

None of this should undermine the appropriate use of authority by adults. But it may need to be exercised in a different way. Ideally, it should be clear what is expected by way of consultation with children as a standard for all staff to meet. It shouldn't depend solely on the whims of individuals but be embedded into the school's ethos. Some schools have appointed someone to do it, or identified a governor who has a specific responsibility for pupil participation, but that risks suggesting that all the other staff and governors don't need to.

It is sometimes difficult in practice, but we do know that the educational problems of disadvantaged and disaffected children and young people will not be resolved without them being part of it. We can't deliver for them, which means that ultimately we have to find a way of engaging them if we are to avoid endless frustration. I can only suggest that if what we are doing now isn't working for them or for us, stop doing it and try something else! In end there might just be another way.

Parents

Parents have more influence on educational attainment, especially for younger children, than almost anything we can do in school. But the cosy world of DfES publications in which everyone appears to work happily together to promote their children's best interests, may not always match the reality. Parents may have all kinds of 'rights', but some choose not to exercise them. Some do not know how to do so and some interpret such language as entitling them to behave as they wish. Schools have all kinds of 'duties' but some operate by informal assumptions and values that may effectively exclude large numbers of parents from participation. Such experiences lead only to a drawbridge mentality, across which schools and parents view each other with ever-increasing suspicion.

Parents who had bad experiences when they were at school may assume that the same attitudes apply equally to their own child's teachers. There will certainly be issues of class, race, language and gender that create barriers in the eyes of many parents. Some may feel reluctance or aggression at the very suggestion that they visit the school, come to a meeting or speak to a teacher. Not all parents understand that this might be expected of them. These feelings may not be considered entirely reasonable and it may be hard for professionals to see things from their point of view. There are several contexts in which such misunderstandings may occur:

Attendance and behaviour

Not all children attend school regularly or behave as we would want. Some never do anything regularly; their lives are full of disorder and chaos. Their family may not plan ahead, nor be able to anticipate problems. They may be juggling incompatible expectations, of which going to school is only one. It may be only the children who are expected to get up and out by a given time in the morning. Going to school most of the time, or only a little bit late, or not getting into a serious argument with a teacher today may represent a considerable achievement. We may have all kinds of critical feelings towards the parents in these circumstances, but we can never really understand the reasons why things are as they are. Mental health issues, family violence, bereavements, financial problems, etc. may all be relevant How might any of us react in such situations?

Any approach to problems like these will require sensitivity, understanding and, above all, flexibility. Inclusive schools empower their staff to be adaptable, not rigid in their approach. When there is something you want to achieve, like improved attendance or better behaviour, giving a family a choice between all or nothing simply creates further conflict. If parents are to be helped to see that education is important, they may need to be offered solutions to the other difficulties that are getting in the way. Threats just add more problems.

Try asking yourself questions such as:

- 'Why should these parents feel positive about the school?'
- 'What is the child missing when they're not here?'
- 'What are we actually offering them?'
- 'What stops them responding?'

Offer a choice between two acceptable options to get things moving. Maybe 50 per cent of what the school wants is sufficient at the moment, together with other strategies to try and move things along in the longer term.

Sending letters home

A significant percentage of parents cannot read, or not at the level at which our letters are sometimes pitched. They may routinely ignore anything that looks official. There may be too many circulars sent home; how are parents supposed to know which ones are important? Does the school recognise the need for minority languages? Some letters are unclear in what they want the parent to do, or present them with ultimatums or cold criticism.

Try imagining what it's like to receive a letter:

- asking you to come to school to discuss your child's behaviour or poor attendance (when you've just come out of psychiatric hospital or split up from your partner);

- asking for money for the school fund or giving details of the school's skiing trip (when you're on Income Support);

- informing you that your child has been excluded (when you're trying to hold down a job and don't know how you will cope when he's at home all day).

If it can be avoided, nothing important should ever be conveyed by standard letter. Some parents may live only five minutes' walk away but no one from the school has ever knocked on the door. Can what you want to say be said in person, and then written down in way that the parent understands and which takes account of their views as well? Can the communication be both ways, rather than being seen as simply requiring the parent to respond to what the school has initiated? If parents don't respond to letters, find out why – there may be something wrong with the letter.

Parents' evenings

Parents have a right to meet with their children's teachers. However, some dread the very idea. This may be because they don't want to hear bad news (especially in front of other parents), or because they see school as an intimidating and alienating place that isn't for the likes of them. Often parents' evenings offer little confidentiality, no clear purpose to why parents and teachers are meeting and a lot of waiting around or frequent repetition which just gets people irritated. It is probably better for parents to see fewer staff for a longer time than a whole series of quick appointments.

It is always worth considering the provision of refreshments, displays, musical entertainments, etc., to make the evening more enjoyable. Try to arrange parents' evenings at a time when parents can best attend – late afternoon or early evening can be a very inconvenient time for parents with small children; later might be better just now and again. It may be worthwhile offering alternative individual times to meet. Target-setting days are all very well but not everyone can take time off work in the daytime. A few parents might need the teacher (or someone else from the school) to go to them instead. A meeting at the home will be time well spent if it's the only way it would ever happen.

'Absent' parents

Increasing numbers of children don't live with all those entitled to be involved in their education. Many fathers, for example, will still have 'parental responsibility' under the Children Act 1989 on an entirely equal basis with the mother, unless they were never married and have not obtained it. This exception too, however, will end as children born after 1 December 2003 enter the school system. Being named on the birth certificate is now sufficient to give you permanent legal status. A divorced parent will nearly always have the same legal rights towards the child as any other parent. It is vital to check, for every child, exactly who the school needs to be involving as a 'parent'. Some may be strangers to the school, not on the database, live elsewhere and just turn up unexpectedly, or are in conflict with their former partner or the child. They may not be around because nobody has told them what school their child goes to.

But most parents will still have every right to be consulted. Very few will be restricted by court orders. Not living with your children does not mean being excluded from their lives. Parents can feel very hurt when important decisions are made without them or when they have never been informed about the child's attendance, for example. Many parents dismissed as uninterested may not be aware of what's going on. They weren't invited to the meeting, sent a copy of the report or given a chance to take part. They may not be interested, but don't just take the other parent's word for it. Some will need special opportunities to visit the school outside the normal times or to receive more than the usual information by post.

There are plenty of other potential flashpoints:

- differences in disciplinary, moral and cultural standards between school and home;
- disputes over how teachers feel about what the parent has allowed the child to do at home or how the parents feel about how the child has been treated at school (made worse if the school has no proper complaints procedure);
- parents with learning difficulties or with alcohol and drug problems;
- times when the school has to take a critical view and when the parent is clearly in the wrong, which will need careful handling to avoid the relationship breaking down entirely.

However, so much depends on the kind of climate created, especially whether parents feel part of the school or not. Has this ever been considered as a school management issue and have strategies and plans been put into place to try and improve things?

PRACTICAL STRATEGIES TO TRY

1. Try drawing up a 'Parents' Charter' which sets out what parents can expect from the school and what the school can reasonably expect from them in return. Don't just involve the easy parents: deliberately include the views of those who might be critical or who would just ignore it if you post it out cold. Involve the pupils, the local community, the voluntary groups. Keep it simple and review it regularly. Make sure it's not all one way, stating only what the parents must do. Include a procedure, independent of the school, for sorting out disputes. Be open to suggestions; talk to people about the school; don't wait for them to come to you. Make sure that the Charter is owned by the teachers and governors and actually put into practice. Change it if it doesn't work. Ask the parents what stops them from getting involved with the school and listen to what they say.

2. Look at how the resources of the school can be used to help the parents, especially those whose own education was unsuccessful. Much of the time it feels like the other way round; large institutions that appear to have huge budgets and well-paid professional staff are always asking the parents to help them. This may make people in disadvantaged circumstances very angry. Extended schools offer a whole new opportunity, and not just for the pupils. How can the school be used to help the whole community, not just with recreation but with education? What skills do the parents have that could be developed alongside their children's? How

could the school enhance the literacy, numeracy and social skills of the neighbourhood, to everyone's advantage? Parents will feel much more involved if they are benefiting too. Their children will be more positive and the culture will be one which encourages participation rather than putting barriers in people's way.

Parent partnership

Local authorities will all have a Parent Partnership Service, often managed and run at 'arm's length' or even contracted out altogether to an independent provider. This service will aim to support the involvement of parents, especially where their children have special needs. Most will extend their functions to children who are excluded and others who are experiencing difficulties in their relationship with schools. They will offer parents impartial advice and information and may run parents' groups, workshops, training days and other events. Some support parents during the exclusion procedure or at SEN Tribunals.

It is always difficult for services like these to engage with those who need them the most. They can sometimes risk becoming a voice only for the more articulate middle-class parents, but they should be keen not to miss those whose voice may not have any other means of expression. It will always be helpful if school staff can promote the existence of parent partnership and try to build bridges wherever possible.

Parenting initiatives

There are numerous programmes around through which schools and local authorities can promote more effective relationships with parents and, crucially, help them to become more effective in their parenting. That's the longer term 'Every Child Matters' goal that results from parents 'making a positive contribution' too – helping to ensure that their children are healthy, stay safe, enjoy and achieve and then go on themselves to be more secure economically. Building better working relationships with parents, especially those on the margins, is a means to an end, not only the end in itself. But school is so important in children's lives that, if things are not working well there, there is inevitably a significant impact on other areas of the child's life as well.

Not everything, of course, actually has to be done by teachers, though they will surely benefit as a result of what is achieved. With the growing emphasis on multi-disciplinary working, other professionals from health or social care may be able to take the lead in managing and delivering these initiatives, within the overall context of a multi-purpose or extended school. Many programmes will work best in Early Years settings.

But it is impossible to overstate the importance of what schools and others can do for the long-term benefit of society and its future citizens by helping people to be better parents. A Parenting Contract, for example, may become a very negative experience, if nothing much is on offer other than 'try harder'. The four schemes outlined below may not be available everywhere but they have a proven track record in making a difference.

Family Links/nurture

Founded in 1997, Family Links is an Oxford-based charity which has now grown into a national organisation (www.familylinks.org.uk). In partnership with Early Years and school settings, and using a network of regional trainers and local area co-ordinators, it offers in particular the Nurturing Programme. This is a 10-week course aimed at parents and children up to and including Key Stage 2. The Nurturing Programme provides a framework for building children's social, emotional and behavioural skills and encouraging an emotionally healthy environment. It creates a framework for citizenship education, supports the aims of the National Healthy School Standard and is endorsed by the DfES through the programme for social and emotional aspects of learning (SEAL).

The topics and weekly activities are set out in handbooks aimed at different ages, supported by games and other resources which do not require extensive preparation once the facilitator is familiar with them. The four 'constructs': (a) self-awareness and self-esteem, (b) appropriate expectations, (c) positive discipline, and (d) building empathy, seek to build the child's 'emotional intelligence' or 'emotional literacy'. This should then promote more positive relationships with those who care for them. In effect it promotes better parenting by helping children to understand themselves better and therefore to deal more effectively with the inevitable frustrations and fears that may interfere with a healthy family life.

Family Links also offer the Parent Programme, a course for parents and carers themselves. Based on the same principles, the topics aim to build on parents' existing skills and introduce new ways of improving family relationships and managing the behaviour of children of all ages. The Parenting Puzzle encourages parents to understand themselves better and gives practical support in helping them to learn to feel good about both themselves and their children. For parents who feel stuck in an endless spiral of conflict and disappointment with their children, the course can offer an opportunity to step back and consult the manual, rather than just blundering on in the vain hope that things will eventually get better.

Triple P

This is a programme from Australia, the Positive Parenting Program, that has been taken up by several local authorities in the UK as well as in various other countries around the world (http://www.pfsc.uq.edu.au/). It has been the subject of several TV documentaries on working with challenging children. It was developed by Professor Matthew Sanders and his colleagues from the Parenting and Family Support Centre in the School of Psychology at the University of Queensland. It aims to:

- enhance parents' skills, knowledge and confidence;
- promote nurturing and non-violent environments for children to grow up in;
- reduce child abuse and the risk of future social exclusion through homelessness, drug misuse, etc.; and
- enhance the mental health of both parents and their children.

The programme was originally intended for those with pre-adolescent children but has subsequently been adapted for use with parents of older teenagers. Work with parents is set within a five-stage context, with various resources attached to each stage:

1. Universal Triple P – media-based information campaigns aimed at all parents, especially though health promotion routes, helplines, print and electronic media.

2. Selected Triple P (and Teen Triple P) – provision of specific advice on how to deal with common child development issues and minor behavioural problems. May involve face-to-face conversations or seminars.

3. Primary Care Triple P (and Primary Care Teen Triple P) – a programme for parents over four sessions, often managed by a health professional or other trained facilitator, teaching specific skills and combining advice, rehearsal and self-evaluation. (This is the level at which a school-initiated programme might be best placed.)

4. Standard, Group, Group Teen and self-directed Triple P – 8–10 sessions offering intensive training in positive parenting skills and enhancement strategies. Offers individual, group and self-directed elements. (A more specialised course to which school staff might be able to make referrals in their local area.)

5. Enhanced Triple P – An individually tailored programme for families with specific problems of dysfunction, relating either to child or parent, such as depression, conflict and anger management. (Again such a targeted group might be available for referrals for schools.)

The programme also offers specialist interventions working with parents of children with a disability (Stepping Stones), and those whose children are at risk of maltreatment (Pathways), though these may not be so readily available. If Triple P does not appear to be available in your local authority, it may be worth discussing what it has to offer with key advisors and local children's service managers. With the new 'joined-up' approach to service delivery, this may be an ideal vehicle for education, health and social care professionals to work together on an integrated approach to addressing parenting issues rather than adopting a more narrow school-centred focus in isolation.

ContinYou/'Share'

ContinYou (http://www.continyou.org.uk/) is a community learning charity that offers a range of resources to tackle inequalities and build social inclusion. It is aimed at providing fresh opportunities for those who have gained least from their previous formal education and training. This includes services based in extended schools, lifelong learning and adult education, health improvement and the regeneration of communities. In particular it offers 'Share' in over 100 local authorities, a practical, hands-on approach to involving parents in their children's learning, across all Key Stages. This is intended to improve the attainment of both children and their parents and to enhance the vital role that parents can play in supporting what happens in the classroom. 'Share' can only be provided by a trained facilitator, in partnership with one or more schools.

Parents and carers are helped to work with their children at home using a range of materials that complement the formal curriculum, linked to the literacy and numeracy frameworks. The emphasis is on a shared learning experience; communicating the excitement of learning, rather than on specific tasks such as spelling or maths, for example. Central to the approach is the accreditation system developed through the Open College Network. This means that parents can gain accreditation for the work they put into supporting their child's learning. For example, they might gain recognition for designing a game based on a theme in one of the 'Share' books or for completing a certain number of units. The facilitators support the parents by running initial meetings, structured group sessions or a self-supporting parents' group. There are also 'Share' message boards on their website so that parents can be part of an on-line community.

The Parenting Clinic

This is a resource pioneered by Carolyn Webster-Stratton at the University of Washington, USA (http://www.son.washington.edu/centers/parenting-clinic/). It has been used by some child and family health services in the UK and aroused considerable interest in government circles. It is a therapeutic approach to behavioural problems that seeks to promote 'social competence', primarily among families with children under 10. Webster-Stratton describes the approach as 'English Parenting'. It is based on her own English mother's 'mothercraft' techniques: firm discipline, clear limits and boundaries, but, at the same time, a strong sense of working together as a family team. Her father, too (who incidentally invented the 'squeegee' mop), transferred the principles of his business to family life. He believed that high-quality 'products' could best be achieved by working in a collaborative way and by supporting and valuing all those involved in the enterprise.

The Parenting Clinic, set up in 1982, has become an international sponsor of a number of intensive and group-based programmes under the general title of 'The Incredible Years' aimed at parent-training, teacher-training, problem-solving and anger management. For children, the emphasis is on simplicity and fun, such as Dinosaur School and a puppet called Wally. For the work with parents there is a strong emphasis on recognising the influence of factors that have an adverse affect on learning. English readers would recognise many of these as social inclusion issues, such as poverty, lone parenting, mental health problems, substance misuse and relationship difficulties. The intention is to build the parents' capacity to be more protective, sensitive and positive about their role, enhancing the use of non-violent methods of discipline in stressful situations.

Conclusion

It is always easier to carry on with the way things are rather than trying something new. But as someone said, if you carry on doing what you have always done, you carry on getting what you have always got – and that is not at present enough for all our children, or indeed for ourselves. We want more. Only a little over half of all our young people achieve the standard of 5A★–C at GCSE. A significant percentage achieve much less and about 5 per cent achieve virtually nothing (including those who are not even entered). Poor outcomes at school have been perpetuated across too many families and communities for too long. They are passed on like precious heirlooms from parent to child with no one really expecting anything to be much different. Teenage pregnancy is too high and too many young people see the status offered by involvement in drugs or crime as the easiest answer to their perceived lack of opportunity. Too many parents have given up on their children, and on own their capacity to do much about it.

We may think that we know what works with families like these, or more likely, what doesn't work, without necessarily seeing the need for further innovation. Many teachers and others may feel that they have already done everything possible to make a difference. That is entirely understandable. We all run out of steam sometimes and we often leave our interventions too late for them to have much impact. More modest achievements in this area are often given little reward compared with the more universally accepted definitions of 'success'.

But I would finish only by reiterating what I hope has been clear from the beginning of this book. All our children deserve the very best of what we have to offer. Even if we're not sure that they always deserve it, they still need it, and they need us to make it available. They deserve the best possible services, and the very best of people working in them. The achievement of the five outcomes of the Children Act 2004, if this is to be anything more than empty aspirations written on endless strategies, policies, plans and other documents that no one ever actually reads, will require us to change ourselves as well as those we are trying to help. Standards have to improve even further; their standards and ours.

As mentioned earlier, part of the government's strategy is an enhancement of the children's workforce. If every child matters, so does every person who works with them, not for themselves, but because of the vital importance of what they do. The media loves to knock social workers, teachers and other 'do-gooders' (surely one of the most offensive terms ever invented), but it would soon miss us if we weren't here. I am convinced that the next best step forward is for all of us who do this valuable, if often under-appreciated work, to borrow some of the enhanced self-esteem offered through the programmes outlined above. We each need to recognise that our own contribution is immensely important. Perhaps it will then be seen in a better light by those in the wider society on whose behalf we do it.

This approach is essential if we are to have any hope of encouraging wider participation by those who currently feel excluded. We have to be clear about our own moral purpose and motivation or they will easily spot that we don't really mean it. We have to set ourselves the highest possible professional standards not be lured into thinking that something less than our best is good enough. We have to make the systems work for difficult children and parents, not find a way round them that solves our problem but still leaves them on the outside. If we do not believe in what we are doing, what difference can we hope to make? Negativity is a killer. It creates its own self-fulfilling prophecy that nothing can ever be done about all these problems so nothing ever is done. That's how many of the families we work with got into such a mess in the first place.

But everything you do, every day, to engage with the parent or child who is easily ignored, or who will happily self-exclude given the opportunity, is your contribution to a healthier society filled with healthier children, adults, families and communities. In the end it is best for us all. Positivity is infectious too and the more productive the contributions that we can make, however modest, the better the hope of increased social inclusion further down the road. It is worth it. If we stop believing that, we are lost indeed.

References and resources

Government publications

All DfES documents are available via http://www.teachernet.gov.uk/

Chief Secretary to the Treasury (2003) *Every Child Matters*. London: TSO (The original Green Paper on the future of Children's Services).

DfES (2006) *Care Matters*. London: DfES.

DfES (2006) *Improving Behaviour and Attendance: Guidance on Exclusion from Schools and Pupil Referral Units*. London: DfES.

DfES (2006) *Keeping Pupil Registers*. London: DfES.

DfES (2006) *Safeguarding Children and Safer Recruitment in Education*. London. DfES.

DfES (2006) *Supporting Looked-After Learners*. London: DfES.

DfES (2006) *Working Together to Safeguard Children*. London: DfES.

DfES (2005) *Pupil Attendance and Absence Management in School and LEA MIS Systems*. London: DfES.

DfES (2005) *New Relationships with Schools: Next Steps*. London: DfES.

DfES (2005) *A National Conversation about Personalised Learning*. London: DfES.

DfES (2005) *Advice and Guidance to Schools and Local Authorities on Managing Pupil Attendance*. London: DfES.

DfES (2005) *Guidance on the Common Assessment Framework*. London: DfES.

DfES (2005) *Common Core of Skills and Knowledge for the Children's Workforce*. London: DfES.

DfES (2004) *Every Child Matters: Change for Children in Schools*. London: DfES.

DfES (2004) *Guidance on Education-Related Parenting Contracts, Parenting Orders and Penalty Notices*. London: DfES.

DfES (2004) *Aiming High: Guidance on Supporting the Education of Asylum-Seeking and Refugee Children*. London: DfES.

DfES (2004) *Identifying and Maintaining Contact with Children Missing, or at Risk of Going Missing, from Education*. London: DfES.

DfES (2003) *Ensuring Regular School Attendance*. London: DfES.

DfES (2003) *Aiming High: Raising the Achievement of Gypsy/Traveller Pupils – A Guide to Good Practice*. London: DfES.

DoH (2006) *What to Do if You are Worried a Child is Being Abused*, London: DoH.

Key websites

National Strategy and National Programme for Specialist Leaders of Behaviour and Attendance: http://www.dfes.gov.uk/behaviourandattendance/

For advice, case studies and regulations on school attendance: http://www.dfes.gov.uk/schoolattendance/

For child protection circulars: http://www.dfes.gov.uk/safeguardingchildren/

For all ECM guidance and documents: http://www.everychildmatters.gov.uk/

For access to all government publications: http://www.teachernet.gov.uk/

Books and other publications

Cheminais, R. (2006) *Every Child Matters: A Practical Guide for Teachers*. London: David Fulton.

Cheminais, R. (2005) *Every Child Matters: A New Role for SENCOs*. London: David Fulton.

Mills, C. (2004) *Problems at Home; Problems at School*. London: NSPCC (overview of research on home–school relationships).

NSPCC (2003) *Learning to Protect*. London: NSPCC (Teacher Training Pack).

Ofsted (2006) *Improving Behaviour*. London. Ofsted (HMI 2377).

Ofsted (2000) *Evaluating Educational Inclusion*. London: Ofsted.

Pierson, J. and Thomas, M. (2002) *Dictionary of Social Work*. London: HarperCollins.

Reid, K. (2002) *Truancy: Short and Long-term Solutions*. London: RoutledgeFalmer (contains an extensive booklist of other related publications).

Whitney, B. (2004) *Protecting Children: A Handbook for Teachers and School Managers*. 2nd ed. London: RoutledgeFalmer.

Index